JEWELS

Ears to Hear Series – BOOK 1

Received by
PAMELA A. HARVEY

Edited by Denise Irvine

Jewels
Ears to Hear Series–Book 1

by PAMELA A. HARVEY

Printed in the United States of America.

ISBN 9781498493215

www.xulonpress.com

INTRODUCTION

The triangle of communion began on July 3, 1985 at 6 a.m. in Detroit, Michigan when Pamela Harvey's prayer partner, Jean Perkins, lifted a heartfelt prayer to the Lord and He, in turn, sent His reply to Pam's heart. The triangle of communion was complete. He instructed Pam to pick up a pen and write. She obeyed… and each day for one year she received His messages, sometimes when she least expected, but always when her heart was most prepared to listen.

Not long after that, I met Pam and she shared segments of her journal with me. It immediately reminded me of the book *God Calling*, written in 1932 by two women in England who also claimed their messages were received from the Living Lord. I had no doubt God had again enlisted a messenger to deliver His words.

The Lord instructed me to prepare Pam's messages for publication. Day after day I typed and as I did, the messages came alive. I experienced a spiritual awakening like none before. My eyes began to clearly see God's Hand in my life; my spiritual ears began to clearly hear His Voice. The book was appropriately named *Jewels*. That was 30 years ago.

In 2016 the Lord impressed upon Pam and me to publish *Jewels*... for such a time as this.

His message on December 23 was, "We are in a time when the eyes of many will be unveiled and they will be able to see Me for the first time, hear Me speak to them with recognition for the first time. Show them by example and through the Word how I can cause them to see and hear as they never have before." That is the purpose of this book.

Jewels is a 365-day devotional designed to carry the reader through an entire year. Although all devotions are based on the Bible, some readings are preceded by Scripture while others are not.

Our prayer is that *Jewels* will minister to each reader in an enlightening, personal way.

Denise Irvine

DEDICATION

To my first-born son,
Albert "Rusty" Curry,
who never scoffed or doubted
when I began receiving these messages,
and is now in a Better Place
with our Lord.
I love you!

JANUARY

January 1

> **Then they will see the Son of Man coming in a cloud with power and great glory. Now when these things begin to happen, look up and lift up your heads, because your redemption draws near (Luke 21:27-28 – NKJV).**

Tell people to get ready for My return, for I am coming soon. There is so much for you to learn and not much time in which to do it. You are experiencing My awesome Presence, My power in bits and pieces or else it would overwhelm you. Remain focused on Me and there will be new experiences that will bring you closer to Me. This is a love relationship – the purest and truest there can ever be. Praise Me!

I would have you do the following: look neither to the left nor the right as you focus on Me. I will show you what is important, what to deal with and how. As long as you maintain that focus, you will be an overcomer in My Name. Very often,

I have given you answers to things without your realizing it and you think it was your own thought. Reaching spiritual maturity is like that. As you grow in Me, you become more aware of Me in everything... My prodding, My direction, My questions, My answers.

January 2

...God has said, "Never will I leave you; never will I forsake you" (Hebrews 13:5 – NIV).

Come one, come all and sit at My Feet as we drink together. Picture us sitting together in the Throne Room for that is the way it is – not separated by millions of miles of space. We are together in earth and in Heaven. Always think of Me as being with you in the closeness of a loving relationship, for there I am.

So many people picture Me as a distant God sitting upon the Throne ready to condemn them if they slip. You must tell them it is not like that. I am the God of love and want only the *best* for My children. Tell them that I am love and truth and would not lie to them. Tell them so that I may tell them personally. It has been taught wrong for so many years, it is an almost impossible task to re-teach them. But, it must be done. Tell them.

January 3

The Trinity – Three in One – cannot be separated. I clearly state in My Word that all three exist and have great importance to My children. Yes, Jesus provides salvation, intercession and advocacy. But, without the two remaining parts, Jesus cannot do His part. The Holy Spirit is necessary for your daily walk – from understanding what you read and what is right or wrong, to walking with power as an overcomer. It is essential. The last/first is Me, God. Without Me at the center responding, coordinating, guiding, reigning victorious, the other two are incomplete. I am the Godhead. I sit at the center of all. I am the Alpha and Omega, the Beginning and the End.

We are very close now. Sit tight.

January 4

It is so much easier to work with My children today than it was with My people of old because I and My Spirit are one and are in you. Therefore, you are able to understand so much more through the revelation of the Holy Spirit than they were able to grasp. In times past, even the simplest of sayings was not understood, for they had not My Spirit within them to clarify. Praise Me and rejoice – for you have the keys to My Kingdom!

Many will come to know Me through the path I have laid out for you. It is a straight path and one in which your direction is clear. Stay on that path. I am with you!

January 5

"Away with you, Satan! For it is written, 'You shall worship the Lord your God, and

Him only you shall serve'"(Matthew 4:10 – NKJV).

I desire a people who are tried and true, who do not flinch at every obstacle. For the work ahead, My Body must be sound/ stable realizing that My adversary is doing all within his power to interfere with My plan.

Therefore, as you meet each obstacle, rejoice knowing that you are being strengthened and purified to better meet your challenges. Know that what you experience is not by chance, but rather to build a more solid you. Rise to all obstacles knowing that I am the Master Craftsman and have designed each moment for your good.

January 6

Man is forever distorting My plan by inserting his limited knowledge instead of being led by Me. I will move a people who are strong in My Word – not just on the outside, but on the inside – who are bold in Me and will take the Word to the world. And, as we move together, My Word will spread with power like electricity.

Too many times there is this outward display, but all too often there is not much happening inside. There is no depth. You must be based in My Word, deeply rooted, so you are able to go forth in seemingly adverse conditions. I say "seemingly" because it never has to be as it seems if you stand on My Word.

It is time for My people to be steadfast, to be overcomers and not shake in their boots whenever they run into a problem.

January 7

Do not plan for tomorrow. Make only the plan that you will serve Me and know Me more today. I know your past, your present and your future. If you but yield to Me and listen to My Voice, you will know that tomorrow will bring the best that I have for you. Trust Me, have faith in Me and rely on Me.

Picture your head resting on My Shoulder as I comfort and protect you. That is how it really is, if you but let Me. Worry not for today or tomorrow. Only yield to Me with an undying love so each step you take is taken with Me. Together… always together.

January 8

Fear not for tomorrow because I am in charge. Continue to focus on Me and all things which have been promised you shall come to pass. I am the Lord your God and I will not allow My work to be deterred. Continue to believe in My good plan for your growth. Continue to confess My power in your life. Strive to have absolute faith in Me, for I have your destiny at hand.

I am bound to love you with all of its intricacies and I am bound to answer your prayers. If you understood this more, there would be little need for fret or worry. Unlike the world, I never change, so I must do what I have said. I *must*.

January 9

The Glory of God is before you. Recognize it in everything you see and touch – the snow, the blue sky, an escape from falling, a winning game, a kind smile, a tender word. I am in you and around you. Recognize Me. When the wind blows, I am there. And with each droplet of rain, I am there. I am everywhere and I am in everything if you but look. My creations are beautiful… only Satan distorts them and brings death and darkness to all he touches. Appreciate everything around you as Mine, and realize the lack of beauty only comes when Satan touches his gnarled hand to it.

January 10

> **Then I saw "a new heaven and a new earth," for the first heaven and the first earth had passed away, and there was no longer any sea (Revelation 21:1 – NIV).**

Every knee shall bow at the Throne of the King. My Kingdom on earth will be a government of love, truth and tranquility… established forever. In the end, My Kingdom will be physically manifested on a new earth. But, for now, it should manifest in the same basic way in the life of each Christian – in business, the family, social activities and particularly churches. There should be no real difference because you have My power and guidance to handle any situations or problems you may encounter. The main difference between the present and the latter days will be a physical manifestation of My Kingdom minus the presence of Satan. With the power I have given you, Satan should not be a threat or a stumbling block.

January 11

I am the Lord your God. I reveal things to you as you need them lest you be overcome. Day by day My plan unfolds. Although you may know the overall plan in generalities, you are receiving essential pieces step by step. Worry for naught, as I am the Master Guide and know all things and work all things together for the best result, if you let Me. Continue to yield to Me and Me alone. Then follow.

There are too many who know of Me and believe in their minds and sometimes hearts what I did for them, but do not know Me at all. No joy. No hope. No love. No assurance. No growth. But through the love and unity of My sons and daughters, their growth will come.

January 12

> **Let us, therefore, make every effort to enter that rest, so that no one will perish by following their example of disobedience (Hebrews 4:11 – NIV).**

There have been many things that have unsettled you as you have walked closer to Me. First, recognize that I am peace and let that peace flow through you. Then, wait for the answer

– My answer. I have many ways of answering and very often the answer is not what you expect. But, as long as you desire to be in My perfect will, the answer will come and it will be correct.

Relax in Me. Often you think you do not have time to wait long for an answer. You think you know the timetable and place undue pressure on yourself with unrealistic goals – goals that are doomed to fail. But, I know the right time, the right place and I am always on time. Relax in Me.

January 13

Take my Hand and walk with Me. Necessities of growth are at hand. Begin to look at yourself more closely, cleansing what you know to be inappropriate and retaining what is based in My Truth. There is no other way, for it is a process of filtering the impurities/scum as a sieve, so that what is left is the meat. As you continue to do this, you will be taken to different levels with different experiences... to more perfectly do My Word/work. You must be clean to truly do My work. Get ready.

My Eyes are your eyes to see, do and share. This gift is not for you alone, but for others to see and be brought closer to Me. See, do, share.

January 14

What do I need from each of you? Your love and desire to do My will. What do I have in return for you? Salvation, power, victory and the greatest love ever offered. It seems such a small price to pay for all that awaits you once you yield to Me. But, make no mistake, although My offer of love stands, time is growing short. There will be a time when it will be too late to say "yes".

Holy, holy! Lord God Almighty! I sit at the right hand of My Father with you in mind, waiting for your call, your confession, your submission, so you first are Mine and I can loose your every prayer in order and on time. Whatsoever is loosed in earth is loosed in Heaven. Use My gift and take your rightful authority over your life and circumstances.

January 15

The test is over time.

Anyone can be jubilant over an exciting occurrence or the ability to minister to another or the proper response to a given circumstance. But the test is over time. Is that joy still there in the quiet of your room when bills are not yet paid or you have been hurt by another or I did not come through for you as you thought I should? The test is over time – when it is just you and Me.

When I talk to you, it is so that others will know that I communicate, by My Holy Spirit, with everyone who wills it. Not just on paper, but at all times throughout the day. I am never away from you except when you shut me out. Imagine! And, why would you shut Me out – Someone who exists for your existence? Why? Ask yourself and see that it does not happen because there is nothing worse than being out of fellowship with Me.

January 16

Your responsibility is to share My Word with My children. If they choose not to listen, it is their choice. But, I have given you the charge to take My Word to all who do not know Me – My first chosen and the children of the Gentiles. I do not expect you to cram it down someone's throat, but I expect you to share My Good News with all. Spreading My Word and your walk with Me have nothing to do with your feelings. It is your responsibility, and woe unto anyone who turns their back on My Calling and shares not the Word.

Then shall the eyes of the blind be opened.... Imagine yourself at twilight seeing only shadows of objects, objects/people with no depth or distinguishing feature. That is how many of My children (Christians) are. They are not in total darkness as the unsaved, but they see only shadows of Me, shadows of Me without perceiving the real Me – My light, My power, My depth. Tell them they must seek My Face, so they know what I look like, how I think and Who I am. Tell them.

January 17

There will be different manifestations of My power now, and it should not frighten you or puff you up as it is time for these things to happen. All gifts are to My Glory. I am with you always even unto the ends of the earth and I shall not let *anything* harm you. Allow Me to flow in you, for it is time to bring more lost to Me. It is time.

No matter what the desires of your heart, never let them become your focus. Never let things or persons become your reason for being because I am your center. I will give you the desires of your heart as I have promised, but you must never confuse your priorities. In your walk with Me, who do you think placed those desires in your heart anyway? I do not create something for you to let it take the place of Me. You need no idols, for you have Me.

January 18

Wonder of wonders am I. Do you marvel at My greatness? I love to hear the songs of praise, but there is so much more. Most often, because people see Me on My Throne and understand on a very small scale My all-powerful ways, they keep Me at a distance. But, I dwell in you and am with you in everything, little and big. I am waiting for you to ask, to desire of Me a service no matter how minuscule. That is My relationship with you.

I will serve you as you serve Me. And as you grow to know Me, your love and service will grow as My serving power strengthens you. Service through service. Love through love. It is a puzzle that has already been solved, but you have not put in the pieces yet. Little and big. Littler and bigger. Littlest and biggest.

January 19

[11] And he said, Go forth, and stand upon the mount before the Lord. And, behold, the Lord passed by, and a great and strong wind rent the mountains, and brake in pieces the rocks before the Lord; but the Lord was not in the wind: and after the wind an earthquake; but the Lord was not in the earthquake: [12] And after the earthquake a fire; but the Lord was not in the fire: and after the fire a still small voice (1 Kings 19:11-12 – KJV).

A touch, as the wind blowing by your ear, is sometimes My guidance. Other times, it is as though I have given you a whack on your head it is so clear. And, still at other times, it is a plain "no" at least for the time being. I need you to be alert and sensitive to Me to follow My leading. Your sensitivity, your hearing will only increase as you spend time with Me in sweet communion.

When you are in love and that special person is on the phone, you do not ask who is calling when you answer. Instead, you recognize their voice right away without question. And it is the same with Me as you set aside time to fellowship with Me and nurture your side of our love relationship. So do not doubt, for I am always with you to lead and guide you. You need only to commit yourself to look, listen and love.

January 20

Guard your steps when you go to the house of God. Go near to listen rather than to offer the sacrifice of fools, who do not know that they do wrong (Ecclesiastes 5:1 – NIV).

Praise and honor are due Me. I am the best friend you can ever have, but I am to be revered. People often view Me in one of two extremes… as some distant omnipotent God or as a friend whom they can use without satisfying My requirements. Yes, I am all powerful. Yes, you can ask Me for anything, but with respect and most of all with love.

Love for Me first and for others is the life-blood of our relationship, for without it, you have nothing. And, from that love, all else will spring – respect, honor, honesty, service. I can do all things, but only when the basic intent is correct. Never underestimate the importance of true love.

January 21

[54] Coming to his hometown, he began teaching the people in their synagogue, and they were amazed. "Where did this man get this wisdom and these miraculous powers?" they asked. [55] "Isn't this the carpenter's son? Isn't his mother's name Mary, and aren't his brothers James, Joseph, Simon and Judas?" (Matthew 13:54-55 – NIV).

When I was young, people thought I was different. But they did not know just how different until later. That I came to save them was particularly incomprehensible/unfathomable especially for those who knew Me as a boy and thought the carpenter's son would never amount to anything. But, little did they know the plan God had for Me.

And so it shall be for you as time goes on. Those who knew you before will not know you now, nor will they expect greatness from you. At times, even you look back and wonder at the changes you see. But, you are to continue without being discouraged, for if others are to be saved, you will be the one to plant the seed.

January 22

> **Then the eyes of the blind shall be opened, and the ears of the deaf shall be unstopped (Isaiah 35:5 – KJV).**

There is much work to do and so little time in which to do it. Hear My Voice and ready yourself for action. There are many who know Me/God but have many misconceptions about their walk as Christians. Show them gently at times and firmly at others. These misconceptions must be corrected because they are stumbling blocks that bind other Christians and keep them from walking as I intended.

Draw these people in for they are lost, although in a lesser way than the unsaved who know Me not at all. Do not fear because you will not do it alone. I will guide you and tell you where, when, who and how. All I require from you is that you hear Me and obey.

January 23

Sheep shall come into My fold as they hear My Word. But, they cannot hear except My children preach it, tell it. One lost sheep is worth any/all of your effort. Do not dismay if they appear not to receive My Word. You have done your part by allowing them to hear it – to plant the seed. Others will come to water it.

You *are* your brother's keeper and never think otherwise. Do you think anything is more important than someone else's salvation – you are too tired, too busy, you have other priorities...? But, before you answer, imagine eternal damnation and torment, then answer. You are responsible for one another that all may share in Paradise for Eternity.

January 24

Grant Me your love, for without it I cannot do the things I was meant to do for you. Those who turn away from Me will be destroyed as many of My people were when I came to Jerusalem. I have so much for you. Through Me, you have peace, love, joy, abundance, eternal life – all that your heart desires – only you must grant Me your love. Institute My "House of Love" in your being, in every part of you.

Glory to God! Love and peace on earth... a day when all the Family can gather around My table and feed on Me. Can you picture a world based on love and peace? No strife, no worry, no darkness... just light. With the havoc Satan has wreaked on earth, it seems an almost impossible vision to grasp. But, that is the way it should always have been and will be soon... soon. Do not lose sight of the Light which is to come.

January 25

Something beautiful is about to happen. You have created the vacuum and I am filling it. And, so it shall be in My Kingdom. You cannot get more until you use what you have. It is the law of the universe. As you use more (create a vacuum), more shall be given unto you (the vacuum will be filled). As you share My Word, more will always come to you. As you learn, a hunger for more knowledge, wisdom and revelation will come. Give and it will be given unto you. Do not, however, let material things become your focus.

Waste not, want not. Everything that is given to you should be turned around for the Glory of God. I have never intended for you to hoard the gifts I give to you. I have always intended that you would share with others and expect to be refilled.

January 26

I am God Omnipotent... Creator of Heaven and earth and all things in between. I sit over all things, see all things and know all things. Yet, I am as putty when I see My child saved (finally believing), loving Me first then others, praising and rejoicing in Me. I am the Great I Am who is here to serve you and to fellowship with you. I Am that I AM. I am the Lord your God. I am your Father. I am all things. As long as you focus on Me and walk in faith (trust Me), I can be all things to you. Even when you slip, even when you fall, I work all things together for good because I know you love Me. Allow Me to be your all now and forever.

January 27

Hallelujah! Hallelujah! Make a joyful noise unto the Lord!

You are as an instrument in which your praise of Me is music to My Ears and all of Heaven rejoices with Me. Whether it is in song, dance, thought or word – it matters not, for it is the most precious sound to Me. Never underestimate the value of your praise because it not only ministers to My Heart, it is a most powerful weapon against My enemy (Satan) and he is powerless against it. Why? Because I inhabit your praise. I dwell in your praise and offer you everything you need – protection, health and healing, freedom, blessings and even joy – that joy that is your strength.

When you praise Me, you are testifying that I am your God and you are submitting to Me, inviting Me into your life. Satan has no choice but to flee because He cannot occupy the same space as I do. Realize the importance of praise and set your heart and mind to establish it firmly in your life. Then praise Me! Hallelujah!

January 28

Haughty eyes... (Proverbs 6:17 – NLT).

In our relationship, I must be your ego. There is no place for your ego in My Kingdom because it means you care more for you than you care for Me. It means if you have a difficult decision to make, what you think will be of benefit will take priority over Me. It means that pride in your abilities will take precedence over Me. I hate pride. And in the end, it means you will rebel against Me if only in the slightest way. Disobedience, large or small, is rebellion.

I urge you to strive to cultivate a humble heart in all situations, for there is no other way. Then you can reach true glory, My Glory – the Throne Room. It is so vast and has room for *all* to sit with Me, to fellowship with Me, to praise and worship Me continually. Imagine!

Glory, glory, glory! Lord God Almighty!

January 29

I will guide you in all things – not just the big things when your back is against the wall, but *all* things. If you seek Me and listen for My answer, your back will not be against the wall because it will not be viewed as such. When you are truly seeking Me, you know that all things work together for good to those who love Me and, that I have made a way out for you. Therefore, your faith in Me will not allow you to be at your wit's end because I bring you peace, joy and salvation. Rest in Me and let Me guide you at each point. Then, you will know the true joy of living and walking with Me.

We want to rejoice and sing! Let the angels rejoice, for that is what they do with each victory no matter how small. Let the heavens ring more and more!

January 30

I am the Lord thy God. Let no one say that he is I. Many gods arise out of a preoccupation with things. Anything that takes your attention from Me and on which you rely, can become a type of god. It does not have to be a graven image as was the case with the children of Israel in times past. It only needs to be, as I have said before, people worshiping whatever it is. That is what money is to so many people – the dollar for the dollar's sake. People relying on the Lotto or their jobs or their status and becoming so focused, it often consumes them. To do something for a higher purpose which is in line with My Word is fine. But to do something and rely on it for *it*, is totally different. Do not be deceived. Look to Me, your God.

What would you like of Me? Simply ask and believe you receive it.

January 31

My Glory is in each of you if you but realize it. If you think of Me as being in you at all times, you would not do half of the things you do. I know it is almost impossible to grasp how I, the God of all, dwells within you, but believe by faith.

Before My Son gave His Life on the cross, He said He must go so He could send the Comforter – God the Holy Spirit – who would guide you into all truth, empower you and live within you. So today, He/We, in all the Glory of Heaven dwell within you with holiness, love, purity, peace, power... all Glory. Think on this and begin to walk as My true child – righteous and upright recognizing Whose you are and who you are. And, know that as your all-seeing Father, I love you more than life – even knowing all about you.

FEBRUARY

February 1

> **And now abide faith, hope, love, these three; but the greatest of these *is* love (1 Corinthians 13:13 – NKJV).**

My entire relationship with you is built on love... love to not see your errors, love to hold you in My Arms when you fail or are lonely or despondent, love to chastise you when needed, love to leave all to choice so that you come to Me freely. Love is the basis for all. Love... love Me first and love others. Surely you cannot enter My Kingdom without this love – My kind of love.

So many have confused My Love with something shallow. But, My Love is so much more. It is never changing whether you are good or bad. It is so perfect, it caused Me to sacrifice My darling Son to suffer and die for you. This is the love I offer to you and it is the greatest gift in all the world. Receive it without hesitation.

February 2

I am the Lord your God. Do not look to yourself or others to satisfy your needs, but to Me. Only I know and understand the total picture as it concerns you. So, it behooves you not to lean upon your own understanding in your daily walk.

I am the Lord your God. Let nothing take My place. When you put Me first in your life, all things will fall into place. I have told My children this for thousands of years and they have continued to listen with a deaf ear. Take My Word to the populace because time is growing short. My way is the only way, the *right* way. Tell them.

February 3

Do not fret or worry. Be anxious for nothing. When I said I came to save, I meant not only from death to eternal life, but I also save you from the hurt, pain and worry of your day-to- day life. "I save" is what I do in a broad sense/interpretation, not in the narrow way that people think of Me. I save... I save you... I save. Release your restrictive thoughts of Me and know that I save in the truest, purest sense. I save. And, as you understand more of what I save you from, you will find a newer freedom and rest in that knowledge. You will know there is nothing to fear because I have saved you and made you victorious over anything you may encounter if you but trust Me and My purpose.

February 4

Then shall the eyes of the blind be opened…

Do not be too hard on yourself when you do not feel you have overcome in the manner you should. Each experience brings you a step closer to Me. It is part of My training ground… to recognize strengths, weaknesses and growth. Do not ever be discouraged. If I am not discouraged, why should you be?

None of it is a surprise to Me the all-knowing, for I sent My precious Son to die for you. You are Mine with all your lumps, bumps, blemishes and imperfections. I knew it all. I knew what I was doing and I knew what I was getting. And, I still chose to work out My good plan in you. Do not look back – just seek Me. I am the Master Craftsman Who molds and makes. Put your trust in Me.

February 5

Precious Blood!

My precious Blood covers all indiscretions when you are truly full of remorse and seek forgiveness… when your heart is right. So many do not understand the importance of My Blood and how it washes, not just at communion once a month or once a day, but continually. I want everyone cleansed or there would have been no reason for Me to die. I died so that all may be with Me.

My Blood is like a wave in the sea washing upon a sandy shore. Each time the wave hits the shore, it takes some sand with it and leaves something else there… a stick, seaweed or an empty can. With Me, My Blood takes all the dirt, filth and sickness, and leaves a purer whiter you... cleansed each time you slip, realizing you will do, can do, and must do better next time. My Blood... cleansing you like the sea.

February 6

Today will be the best day of your life. Why? Because you will be with Me. Each day grows better and better when you spend it with Me – not by looking at your circumstances and challenges, but by looking at Me. The so-called dryness you may feel is only the calm before manifestations break forth unlike any experienced heretofore.

Do not be fearful. Only trust in Me at each step. You still have the tendency to plan and handle things more than I desire. As you learn to rest in Me, it will bring you to a new level, a new plateau.

February 7

Tame the shrew in you and do not allow your agendas, attitudes or stubbornness direct you. You do not know what I have planned as each day is a big day for no other reason than I planned it. Do not undercut it. Love and joy and peace must be the focus of the day. Take each day at a time, knowing nothing has been left to so-called luck and I have ordered all.

I will give you the desires of your heart, but it shall not be in your time but Mine. So often, the greatest plans are thwarted or at the very least delayed because you want it done in your time, which is imperfect time. By taking each day at a time while resting and trusting in Me, you will have your heart's desire in the right way and *right on time*.

February 8

Woe unto you, scribes and Pharisees, hypocrites! For ye are like unto whited sepulchers, which indeed appear beautiful outward, but are within full of dead men's bones, and of all uncleanness (Matthew 23:27 – KJV).

East and west will be as one when My Kingdom is set up on earth. There can only be oneness in My Kingdom – oneness with Me first, then oneness with your brothers and sisters. Anything that causes separation – from Me, from them – must be done away with as there is no place for it. I have repeatedly told you this, but until you really examine yourself, you will never realize how what seems very small can cause this separation. Be aware that the enemy wants nothing more than to steal and distort our oneness because it gives him fertile ground in which to do his dirty work. Be alert to his tactics and give him no place to thrive.

February 9

(As it is written, I have made thee a father of many nations,) before him whom he believed, even God who quickeneth the dead, and

calleth those things which be not as though they were (Romans 4:17 – KJV).

Confession/profession is the key to My power. If you have faith and do not voice this faith, it shall never come to pass. I have created you in My Image and thereby given you power to create with your words/your tongue – to bring life or death, to bring roses from ashes. That is why your words on a day-to-day basis are so important and must be guarded. Your words once spoken call things into being – for good or bad, blessings or curses. Learn to confess My Promises continually and call them into being. Then it shall be My good pleasure for you to reap them.

February 10

I will provide everything you need and desire. Continue to confess My Word and My Promises. They are not given simply to read and talk about on the Sabbath, but to be used and exercised daily. You are to have power as My child and it is time to utilize that power. It is as electricity which is ready for use in the socket, but if you do not put the plug in and turn on the appliance it will just sit as though it does not exist. So it is with Me. Plug into My power and walk with the electricity (the authority and power) of My Promises. Stand tall, head high, and march on.

This is warfare not some laid back game. Equip yourself and go forth, and nothing will be held back from you. Walk, walk, walk… by faith and not by sight. Visualize those Promises in your heart – see them with your mind's eye – and the manifestation is yours! Glory to God!

February 11

This is the day which the Lord hath made; we will rejoice and be glad in it (Psalm 118:24 – KJV).

This is the day that I have made. Rejoice and be glad in it! I have made each day. Find peace and joy in each day as you meet each challenge with the knowledge of your victory.

There are many questions you ask that are due to timing. However, the majority of delays and lack of clarity have to do with walking in the natural as the world walks. Yes, things happen, but the Spirit-man is not to even see these things. As you grow in Me there should be less vacillation between your physical and spiritual awareness. Then as you pray, know that the spiritual realm is the true reality… and the natural is not able to cancel out or affect what has already been solved or won spiritually.

February 12

He answered, "'Love the Lord your God with all your heart and with all your soul and with all your strength and with all your mind'; and, 'Love your neighbor as yourself'" (Luke 10:27 – NIV).

Love for Me first and then your neighbor is My most important commandment, for without love you have nothing. Think of what *I* would do as your Lord in a particular situation and do it. Then, you will truly be walking as I walked and spreading My Love to others. You must never turn your back on others who are in need of My Word and God-love. Let Me clean them up. Your charge is to bring My Love to others by your example and My Word. Concentrate on this principle and run with it!

February 13

My desire has always been for you to trust in Me and *not* in the institutions of others. I did not cause these situations. (Satan always attacks My children in financial areas.) But I have not intervened substantially because you needed to see that nothing is certain except Me. Walk as My child even during these trials.

Wait on Me. Everything must be done in My time. Wait on Me and watch for Me. I will rarely do things exactly as you expect, but they will be done the best way… and right on time.

February 14

> **The thief cometh not, but for to steal, and to kill, and to destroy: I am come that they might have life, and that they might have it more abundantly (John 10:10 – KJV).**

Claim My Promises and stand on them! Do not be deceived by the thief/Satan who seeks to steal and destroy. You may feel that your back is against the wall, but it is only because you do not see the handle on My door that is right beside you. You are taken care of in all things as you seek Me, and all solutions will be provided for you. Do not fret, do not worry, do not be anxious. The door is opening… and beyond it, are the answered wishes and desires of your heart. I died that you might live and live more abundantly! Serve Me.

February 15

> [19] **And He took bread, gave thanks and broke *it,* and gave *it* to them, saying, "This is My body which is given for you; do this in remembrance of Me."** [20] **Likewise He also *took* the cup after supper, saying, "This cup *is* the new covenant in My blood, which is shed for you" (Luke 22:19-20 – NKJV).**

Do these things in remembrance of Me. In all things remember Me. When you partake of My Body and My Blood… remember Me. When you are at work or at play… remember Me. In all things I am there. Do them to My Glory in remembrance of Me. I will never leave you nor forsake you. Even in those very dark periods, I am there. Often you are not listening, but I am there working many miracles in your life. I am always there claiming the victory for you. Never forget. Do all things in remembrance of Me. I died that you might live!

February 16

> **[4] Rejoice in the Lord always. Again I will say, rejoice! [8] Finally, brethren, whatever things are true, whatever things *are* noble, whatever things *are* just, whatever things *are* pure, whatever things *are* lovely, whatever things *are* of good report, if *there is* any virtue and if *there is* anything praiseworthy—meditate on these things (Philippians 4:4, 8 – NKJV).**

This is the day... My Day. This is the day that I have made. Rejoice! Rejoice in all things. Do not participate in or feed negativity. I am the God of love, joy and peace. Therefore, with Me in you, you have My Love, joy and peace at all times. When you see them slipping away from you as you face the day, find time to quiet yourself and spend time with Me. I will replenish you. Then, act accordingly.

Power... Action... Glory. You know that it is all Mine. Therefore, because I can do anything, take the keys to the Kingdom and run!

February 17

If you are truly walking in faith, you must not only confess your faith and believe it is so, you must act. Act it. For how can it be so if you act contrary to what you say? That is an element so many people forget in their walk with Me. Their actions must be an extension of their faith after confessing it. You cannot say you are a millionaire and then act as though you are a pauper and have only a dime left. You must take action with wisdom in My Kingdom – action! Belief, confession, action. And if you truly believe, your actions will be a natural outgrowth of what you say and believe. You cannot claim victory and live in defeat.

February 18

Then shall the eyes of the blind be opened...

Go forth and bring the Word to the flock. The means will be provided for you to do this, so you need not worry about it. You are to teach others, but only with your focus on Me. Do not get antsy, for I am in control. You will know when it is time... very, very soon. Very, very soon. And with whatever you do, know that any embarrassment you may feel at times, is not from Me.

As you walk as I walk and are an example of the love that I have for each one of you, the manifestations of My power in you will break wide open. You would not believe Me if I told you all, but be assured that it is perfect and in order.

February 19

Great day! I am your milk and honey. Never believe otherwise. Many will come and many will go, but only a few are chosen. You are chosen and your work begins immediately.

Heed My Word and direction. I will use you and use you for the Kingdom, but you will never be used up.

Today is the day that I have made. Rejoice! Rejoice and be glad in it! Take My Hand and walk with Me and My guidance will be clear – as clear as a guide dog that leads the blind. They place their complete trust in this animal trained to serve and guide them. How much more do you think I can lead and guide you? Have the faith of the blind as they cross busy streets with their guide dogs. So it should always be with Me.

The children of the Lord shall see My Face and seek Me in everything. Clarity in much is forthcoming.

February 20

> **[6] But let him ask in faith, nothing wavering. For he that wavereth is like a wave of the sea driven with the wind and tossed. [7] For let not that man think that he shall receive any thing of the Lord (James 1:6-7 – KJV).**

I am not a God to be manipulated as I have My own plan/agenda. Although I say that I give you the desires of your heart and I will move mountains for you when you have faith in Me, there is more involved. It does not mean I am to be used at your every whim. I long to bless you, I yearn to bless you. But you must be in tune with My purposes, placing Me first in your heart, mind and spirit. When you set Me first, then your desires are My desires and I will bless you abundantly.

Stop canceling out your answered prayer as soon as you ask. It does not matter that you do not see the way in which it will be answered. It only matters that you believe it will be answered in whatsoever way I will. Your prayers have been answered. Leave it at that.

February 21

I have work for each of you to do no less important than the next. The time has come for My army to move forth and bring "Israel" to Me. Touch each person you meet with Me – not always through words, but often through actions. Time cannot be wasted in spreading My Word. We are in warfare… warfare for souls in Eternity. Just as the Israelites had to take the land I had promised to them; your war has been won. You must go through it to bring about My perfect plan. It may not appear to be easy, but I have thoroughly equipped you to be victorious. Move forward!

February 22

> **Nay, in all these things we are more than conquerors through him that loved us (Romans 8:37 – KJV).**

You have won through the good fight of faith. Your battles are won. Know that. Only your lack of belief can cause you to be defeated. Exercise this power at every step, in every moment. Profession and belief (faith). You are more than a conqueror…

not simply a conqueror, but *more* than a conqueror! Why is it so hard for you to realize this? You believe My Word, but do you only believe the parts that you want? No. Either you believe it all, or believe none of it. So, believe that you have won in all things.

Do not worry about what you see. What you see will come in line with your belief and confession. Do it. Say it now and it shall be yours!

February 23

You will walk as I walk, do as I do and look neither east nor west. Place your focus entirely on Me. Is that such a hard thing to do?

Take My keys and run! They are yours and can open any door, *any* door! Do not focus on the natural. Focus on Me. Have tunnel vision when it comes to Me. I am the only

light you should see at the end. I am it. I am all. Know this and I will supply you with the keys that I have. I am the Master Skeleton Key. Use it, use Me, as you serve Me.

February 24

> **5 Trust in the LORD with all your heart, And lean not on your own understanding; 6 In all your ways acknowledge Him, And He shall direct your paths (Proverbs 3:5-6 – NKJV).**

Do not look to tomorrow. Look to today with right-now faith. Often you limit your blessings by thinking it is too hard for something to happen today. You say, "I can't imagine how God can do it today." But, did I not say all things are possible when you believe? Did I not say that? Well, believe it. When you pray, believe in the now without doubting and I will show you power you have never seen before. And, I will use you to show others. Get ready!

Several times you have almost had it and it slipped away. This time you will get it as it is a learning process. There is no way to get it all at once, so do things step by step as I direct you. You will reach the point you seek in time. You are ready. Manifestations are at hand. Be ready and *trust in Me*.

February 25

You are My child and as your faith has grown, so I shall supply your heart's desire. You are My child and the love which I have for you and all mankind is beyond your understanding. Just imagine the love your mother or father has had for you over the years and multiply it one hundred-fold into infinity. Such is My Love for you… loving you, wanting you to grow, to succeed, to be My vessel. It is this love upon which the entire universe is built – My Love for you, your love for Me, your love for others. *Love*. And so it shall be in Paradise.

Then shall the eyes of the blind be opened…. It is as if an extra sheath, a cataract, has been removed from your eyes so that you can truly see. Rejoice! Take the keys to My Kingdom and run this race as never before!

February 26

This is the day that the Lord has made. Rejoice! It is a most exciting day!

Release all to Me. When you have not, it is because you ask not or you ask amiss. If you have asked rightly, it is done. Leave it. You need not come begging to Me. That is not the relationship we are to have. Ask and believe... and it is done. Come boldly to the Throne Room with reverence and respect, and make your desires known. Your parents would not want you nagging them with repeated petitions, and neither do I. Bless Me.

February 27

Masses will come to Me. The outpouring of My Spirit will be unmatched today and you must have a part in it. I release you to do My work as you are My chosen vessel to do My will. Now watch Me work. Take My keys and run! Through tests and trials come triumph!

Manifestation is at hand. Claim the Promises in My mighty Name and watch Me work them out. Your spiritual gifts will become even more evident as you exercise them in service to Me. You are no longer in a bind. You are no longer tied to a person, place or thing, only to Me. I will meet you soon.

February 28

Nestled in My Arms is how you are to envision your relationship with Me… a relationship in which there is constant touching, constant contact – one touch eliciting another's response. That touch is faith and love – My Love for you and your faith in and love for Me. One brings forth another. See it as a flowing in which you are only limited by your own limits. Then, when you come to understand My Presence and My relationship with you, you will know that in Me you have everything.

February 29

Then shall the eyes of the blind be opened…

Your eyes are opening and you must hang on to the end. So many of My children quit/give up just as they are ready to receive My blessing. So, I challenge you to hang on with no self-pity. Know that I love you, I hear you and I answer you. Celebrate!

I told you I give you your heart's desire – a desire that you will only have through your close relationship with Me. You want for yourself what I want for you. Therefore, you do not have to include *if it be thy will*, for you will know My will from our intimate, all-encompassing togetherness. Remember… we are as one, always touching as My will becomes yours and yours in turn becomes Mine.

MARCH

March 1

Humility and service are what I desire from you. Without them, I cannot fully work through you. Imagine My works through you without proper humility. It would be disastrous because your focus would be on you and the wonderful works *you* do instead of on Me. Be humble and willing to serve – that is the way it must be.

It is time. My message was clear. I placed an idea on your heart and through steadfastness and work, blessings will occur to accomplish the plan. Then, I implore you to serve with humility. It is time.

March 2

Tarnished vessels are dipped in Me/My Blood to bring forth shiny new ones. Realize that I do this for you not because you have done anything to deserve a cleansing, but because I have always loved you and want you free of the darkness and death of this world. Trade the dinginess of this world for the brightness of life with Me. Come to Me.

I died for this purpose. Why do so many of you cheat Me of what I desire to give to you? Why do you cheat yourselves of My precious gift to you? I came so that you might come to Me and have life more abundantly.

March 3

Holy, holy, holy. Lord God Almighty!

So many do not know what they have in Me. They envision Me as some distant God working miracles in times of old or through a few chosen evangelists of today. No, no, no! You must tell them. I use whoever desires Me in their life. I am not a respecter of persons. I have a desire to draw all men unto Me, and work to do so. Tell them I am the same miracle-working God today as in centuries past. I have told you that you would do even greater works this day. Let them know that I never change. So, what I did before, I do now and in the future. Help them to understand what I have for them today. *Right now.*

Go forth in My Name and let nothing deter you. There is nothing more important than My work for you. *Go Forth!*

March 4

Do not try to fit yourself into the molds of others. I will show you what is for you and what fits. Do as I have directed and all ministries will exist peaceably side by side. But, be clear – when one gets too greedy and becomes interested only in self, whatever has been done will have no lasting benefit. It will become counterfeit.

Satan is in many ministries. Be careful and seek My Face because he will try to overtake/devour you as a lion. However, be assured, he will not succeed because you are Mine and now have the keys to the Kingdom!

Worship Me.

March 5

Many mysteries will unfold to you. The more you remain in the Spirit – focused/centered on Me – the more will be revealed. I want to reveal so much to you, but often I am unable to – your focus is not sharp enough, there is too much clutter and your vessel would break or be overwhelmed. Remember that you are in school – My School – and as such you have lessons to learn and homework to do. Some will be easy and some will be hard, but I want to give you a summa cum laude diploma. Persevere and you can receive *all* My blessings.

Doors are opening before you. Be ready and recognize My plan. It is a great one!

March 6

Everything is handled in My perfect time. Do not try to force anything as you know what the only result will be – less than the best. Refresh yourself in Me by meditating on My Word, praying and communing with Me. Then, you will be able to recognize what I give you as opposed to anything Satan sends your way. You have gifts. Use them and know they are from Me. I am ready to increase them to My Glory. Much increase.

Make time for Me and your next step will be in the perfect time and the perfect place. Never underestimate the importance of your time with Me as it has been ordained by Me.

March 7

Yesterday is the past, today is today and tomorrow is tomorrow. Take each day a step at a time with Me. Do not go ahead, do not stay behind. Take each day with Me.

For too long, you have allowed the things of your past to hamper you and hold you back. Understand that each day is a new day with Me, so it is time to release them and let them go. But, at the same time, I caution you not to go ahead of Me. Stay with Me and use the things of your past to propel you into greater works with Me. It is as I have said. Understand that everything you have experienced is never a waste, but to be used for the greater good. Trust Me and trust My masterful guidance.

March 8

Clarity and service.

Keep your eyes off self and look to Me. In this age of self-indulgence and preoccupation, it is of the utmost importance that you do it My way. Leave no question as to who you are in Me and Who you serve. Then shall the eyes of the blind be opened….

There will be rough periods and there will be smooth periods, but know always that you will be triumphant as I am with you. Bring your shallowness to a masterpiece in Christ. I will show you the way out of misery. I will show you the way out of confusion. I will show you the way out of frustration into My peace forever. And, I will shower you with blessings along the way.

March 9

> **Then he said to his disciples, "The harvest is plentiful but the workers are few" (Matthew 9:37 – NIV).**

Work with and for Me as there is much to do. Serve Me and watch My blessings flow to you as you bless others – not that you do things for rewards, but I have promised it is so. I will bless you as it is My desire.

When you are sure the work which you do is My work and not yours, give it your all. I will provide the rest and strength you need. I will give you guidance. I will bless you with whatever you need, for there is no lack in Me.

There is much to do and so few willing workers. Make a decision to work with Me and know the joy of serving Me.

March 10

Do not be deceived, God is not mocked; for whatever a man sows, that he will also reap (Galatians 6:7 – NKJV).

I am the God of all nations. As in the days of old when My people worshipped other gods, it is today. Some actually label it and worship it as God/Me. But, all too often, their god is not recognized as such. They worship money, fame, sex… and do not even realize they have made them gods.

Search yourself and remove those things that hold more importance to you than Me. Allow Me to cleanse your heart of any and all false gods. Then, you will truly have no other gods before you/Me. I am not to be mocked.

March 11

And we know that all things work together for good to those who love God, to those who are the called according to *His* purpose (Romans 8:28 – NKJV).

If you do something believing (truly) that it is from Me and somehow it is not, I have told you I work all things together for good to those who *love* Me. Just continue to look, listen and love. I am the ultimate Mastermind.

Watchful eyes, listening ears, loving hearts – I must have these to do My work through you. And, My work it will be.

I will not reveal all I plan to do, for it is not for you to know nor would you be able to comprehend it all. Just know that I am with you orchestrating this symphony… and what a symphony it is!

Flow with Me. Know that I am in control and it is all part of My plan. All you need do is continue to seek Me by listening, looking, loving and finally, being obedient. Stay in tune.

March 12

Family… unity.

The family must be drawn in. Time is growing nigh for all who are called by My Name to take the Gospel to their families. Yes, you have a responsibility to all, but your family should be a priority in your ministry. (Every child of Mine is in ministry.) Spread the Word. You are a member of your heavenly Family first and your earthly family second. Although I require your devotion first, do not neglect the lost in your earthly one. It is not pleasing to Me when you minister to others and give little thought to your own relatives to the point they are excluded from eternal life with Me. Reach out to those around you, for we are in this together and I desire not to lose one.

March 13

Many will come and many will go, but I am forever. Although I change not, My mercies are new each day.

Your lessons will come faster with each passing day. Know My Voice. Know that I am in charge and follow Me. Your trials are nothing compared to the rewards I have for you. Trust Me and do not fret about anything. I have told you that I am your Shepherd and you shall not want. I have told you that I supply your needs. Bills are needs. I will supply their payment. Do not doubt, only believe. Speak it and know that it is done. I know all and I am in control. Shout it from the housetops and tell the world!

March 14

Do not worry about man-made rights and wrongs, instead, concern yourself with My guidelines/principles. I will give you clear confirmation, then you make your choice. Whoever doubts My Word will not see the true fruit of My work, so believe even when, especially when, your senses tell you the opposite. I know that doubt will come to you because it is the way of the world and what people see takes priority over everything else even if it is a lie. However, My charge to you is to recognize those thoughts, cast them down and exercise the faith I have given to you.

It is often good for the world to be aware of the challenges Christians face so they can also see how differently they meet them with faith. You are My light by living it. As a light draws insects to it without their knowing why, so shall you draw others to Me… but those drawn shall *live* and not die.

Believe. Rejoice today, tomorrow and forever!

March 15

Joy to the world!

There is so much of My joy to be experienced in this life, your present life. Yes, the obstacles will always be there, often as a result of poor choices and the adversary. But, the joy, the blessed joy that I give is still to be evident. Joy in each obstacle. Joy in each blessing. Joy in spreading the Gospel. Joy in all. For when you know I have planned for all and am working all to its magnificent conclusion, how can you have anything other than My joy? How can you? Think about each facet of our relationship, and challenge yourself to find joy in all you do. It is there if you but look.

March 16

> **In the beginning was the Word, and the Word was with God, and the Word was God. [2]The same was in the beginning with God (John 1:1-2 – KJV).**

My Glory surpasses all else. Teach this to others. It matters not what they see, but what they know in their hearts, for what they know will ultimately be what they see. Glory!

Take My Hand and I will lead you to Paradise where all My children are welcome. Be not afraid. I am not like the drug man who gets you hooked on something while professing to only want your good. What I offer is a permanent "high" without anything artificial being placed in you, without taking more from you than you get. What I offer is real… you get much more than you ever pay for. You can never match My giving because I am the greatest Giver of all and I love you. As long as your prayers accompany a right heart and are in line with My Word, I will continue to answer them until you come Home to be with Me.

March 17

Watch carefully and listen to all that is said. Discuss it with Me/My Holy Spirit and read My Word. You will know whether it is right or wrong, for the time is coming when men will look to you for answers and you must tell them the truth… My Truth. Woe to the one who does not tell them My Truth!

Share it all and you shall never be without. Make yourself ready for a higher life in Me. Accept it as it is and know that it is I. Many will come and many will go, but I am forever. Accept no falseness/idols. Know I am the only One True God.

March 18

Mercy is so important to My ministry. I have mercy as you must. You will encounter all types of people who you feel do not deserve mercy, but make every effort to show mercy and it will confound the wise who have only worldly wisdom. Do you deserve mercy? Yet, you always have it.

Believe and others will be caught on your wave of belief. Think of the way the waves of the sea carry all in their path to shore or out to sea. So it is with your belief. Others partake of My blessings through your faith in Me without even being aware of it. Where possible we will let them know.

March 19

> **"...And be sure of this: I am with you always, even to the end of the age" (Matthew 28:20 – NLT).**

Glory to God! I am with you always, even unto the end of the earth and intend to never leave you. That is My Promise to you today and forevermore. At times, you may feel that I have deserted you, but I am not man that I should lie nor would I. I have planned all/sacrificed all for us to be together and it would make no sense to abandon you at any point.

Continue to make periods of quiet time to commune with Me. Otherwise, it will be more difficult to rest in Me and feel My gentle Touch, hear My gentle Voice. Nothing need be left to your own understanding as I am leading you in all areas. Know that. Believe that. Yes. You will have clarity in all things. I am the Mastermind.

March 20

Picture hands together as one bridging differences, similarities, prejudices in My unity. Your focus on Me can only bring unity – love to any and all. My Love can only bring unity and reconciliation. My Love can only bring compassion and forgiveness. My Love can only bring perfection and cannot tolerate anything else. If your love runs contrary to My Love, begin to search your heart to rid yourself of that difference and allow it to be cast out of you for it is poison to you and to those around you.

Did I not send My disciples out two by two? And, so it shall be with you, doing works and wonders with others to My Glory.

March 21

When you come into My House/My Presence, wipe your feet and kick the dust of your past off. I am the God of many mansions, but you cannot enter without knocking on the door and wiping your feet. Many try to bring their dirt into My House, but I will not permit it, for I am your Holy God and accept nothing less.

Last night I was with you, soothing you and holding you. Did you know that? I am peace. I am your peace. I am your peace over troubled waters as a glider over turbulence. Recognize what you have in Me and receive it from this time forth.

March 22

You cannot imagine all that I have in store for you. I tell you this; there is no lack materially, spiritually or physically in My Kingdom. I am in you and around you. What may seem like delays are not so. They are necessary steps now for the perfect timing of My plan. Walk in Me. Walk with Me. Shall I not always be there? It is as I have told you. I am with you always. Do not fear, do not squirm... do not, do not! *Do* rest in

Me, trust Me and love Me. All of the rest will be as it should be – testimonies, manifestations, action, agreement. Lesser things are being completed for the greater works now. Be ready!

March 23

My Love for you is deeper than your heart or mind could ever comprehend. I do not do things to confuse you, but your abilities are not at a point to understand it all nor will they ever be until you are with Me in Heaven. So, trust Me. Realize the depth of love I have for you. (Would you have allowed your loved one – a son, a daughter, niece or nephew – to go through what I did to save people who had no interest in being saved?). You are always in safekeeping with Me because I know *all* and am guiding you at every point, every turn to a higher level. Flow with Me in complete faith and trust.

March 24

Many will come and many will go, but My Love is *forever*... for Eternity. That means you will never be without My Love. So, you must know that misery and pain are not of Me nor are hurt, deception or confusion. They were not My plan for you in the Garden and will never be because I love you too much. They are just part of what you experience as a result of living on this tainted earth and the dastardly plan of the enemy. Never think I send such things, for they are not of Me. I am love. I am peace. I am joy.

March 25

He makes me lie down in green pastures, he leads me beside quiet waters (Psalm 23:2 – NIV).

It is not that you cannot hear Me at times, but that you block Me when you do not hear Me clearly as you think you should. Do not over think your role. I set the guidelines and I am directing you to relax in Me. Do not go ahead of Me. You are and will be ready.

Shall we meet, just you and Me, in some quiet place and revel in the beauty of our relationship? I long for our special time together to love and experience the joy of our togetherness. Take time to commune with Me and allow Me to refresh you on every level.

March 26

[24] Then King Nebuchadnezzar was astonished; and he rose in haste *and* spoke, saying to his counselors, "Did we not cast three men bound into the midst of the fire?" They answered and said to the king, "True, O king." [25] "Look!" he answered, "I see four men loose, walking in the midst of the fire; and they are not hurt, and the form of the fourth is like the Son of God" (Daniel 3:24-25 – NKJV).

Shadrach, Meshach and Abednego. As I was with them, so I am with you. These young men were no more special to Me than you are, but they were committed to Me in a way you have not reached. But, it will come as you continue to strive and hunger for Me, as you make up your mind not to give up or be discouraged. We are only beginning our journey together and have a long way to go with many things for you to learn and do. Continue to focus on Me and remember that I must have your obedience. Then you will see the perfect completion of My plan. We have much work to do in a very short time. All resources are Mine and you shall have them.

March 27

Lessons to learn – small ones, large ones – all are important. Learn them well as you will need them in the future. Nothing is as difficult as it seems. Impatience is the destroyer of so many of My plans and in your impatience, too often you become distracted and lose focus. I have My own timing because I know the beginning from the end and what will happen in between. Understand that what you see and know at any given time is only a miniscule view of what is actually occurring.

Learn to wait on Me. Wait on Me and rest in Me. There are no problems that I cannot handle. In yielding to Me, you yield your problems, your cares, your worries. Lean on Me.

March 28

At that moment the curtain of the temple was torn in two from top to bottom. The earth shook, the rocks split (Matthew 27:51 – NIV).

The veil has been rent, the Holy Spirit has been sent. Little do you know what I have in store for you. Do not even try to guess, for you would only hamper what is to happen. Stay close to Me. Realize I am in you by My Spirit and work through you as I am guiding your steps on every level. Trust Me to work all out in the best possible way at the best possible time.

Necessary steps. In the natural world, you do not leap from the first floor to get to the second. You go up step by step, sometimes skipping one until you reach the next level. In My realm, I order the steps, I order your steps, for I am the Mastermind of My Master Plan.

March 29

Masterful Savior, I am. I have power above all power. I am the Name above all names. There is nothing I cannot and will not do for those who love Me, whether it is healing bodies and minds or finances and situations. I can do it all through those who are willing. Do not think I say these things to boast, but that you would understand Who I am and Whose you are. I am not some weak God that was made with human hands and needs to be carried, nor am I simply the sun or moon or stars that are so magnificent in the heavens. No! I created it all and I am above all. Praise Me and know that I am *He*.

March 30

When I see you, I see your heart and your desire to please, not the intermittent stumbles and falls. Remember, I am there to pick you up, to push you forward, to draw you near. I am there always – with you throughout Eternity. Never fear that you cannot get beyond your past.

All things are not fair. You yourself have even said, "It's not fair, Lord. Why me?" And, as long as you live in this world with the enemy running rampant, there will be trials and tribulations. But, be of good courage because you will overcome by faith and I will work all things together for good to you who love Me. Never give up, for there will be a reckoning on that final day. Never forget that I am your stilt, your cane, your crutch… when it is necessary.

March 31

Remember Me always in all that you do. Put Me first in your remembrance. I am with you to guide you and lead you, but I must be foremost in your mind and spirit. Always. Otherwise, how can I lead you if you are not committed to following?

I am everlasting love – not a flash in the pan. My Love for you compels Me to remain close to you and direct you to your perfect end. Knowing that, surely there can be no one else (no idols) for you. I am the First and the Last. I shall move fast at times and slower at other times. I know the total picture – the total plan – and am working it out for your good. Strive to understand that your care is of utmost importance to Me.

APRIL

April 1

> **Jesus replied, "Truly I tell you, if you have faith and do not doubt, not only can you do what was done to the fig tree, but also you can say to this mountain, 'Go, throw yourself into the sea,' and it will be done" (Matthew 21:21 – NIV).**

Blessed assurance – I am yours. Nothing can separate Me from you except you. We are one, you and I, and together we will move mountains.

Learn patience in your walk with Me. Sometimes, My plan calls for immediate manifestation while other plans take longer to manifest. The difference in time, however, makes one no more true or important than another. Always as you await the manifestations I have promised, the lessons you learn and your spiritual growth make the delay (as you see it) more than worthwhile. Remember that I plan all and if I have promised then it is so, no matter what you see presently.

April 2

Mastery of all things is My forte. You need not try to figure out what I plan to do in any given situation other than to know that it will work to its beautiful/perfect conclusion. Sound hard? Sound confusing? Your answer will only be "yes" if you do not trust Me. Have you forgotten that I am the Beginning and the End? Have you forgotten that I am all-seeing and the I AM? Have you? Well, who better to trust than Me? Think on that and turn your sight to Me because I will never fail you.

Shameless denial of Me will profit no one.

April 3

Shamelessly people distort My Word and shambles are being made of numerous lives because they do not know Me. They read My Word, but half read with little or no understanding. Others barely read and take bits and pieces out of context to fit their fancy while they share their limited knowledge.

We are to turn that around and reveal My true Word. Tell them. Tell them of the love that awaits them. Tell them what beauty and life await them when they come to know Me. Tell them. Time is growing short and there is much to do, so be sure to consult with Me on all things. *All.*

April 4

Then shall the eyes of the blind be opened… and I will come back to reign gloriously. Do you know how long it has been?

Praises be to God! In these last days, My power will be coming forth in untold force as never before. Praise Me! I am the Alpha and the Omega and no one comes unto Me but through My Son. Many try to enter by making their own religion with false gods and guidelines while thinking they know the truth. They are deceived and it will not work. They can only come through the door, My Son, to be a part of My Family. Tell them.

April 5

> **[23] And these three men, Shadrach, Meshach, and Abed-Nego, fell down bound into the midst of the burning fiery furnace. [24] Then King Nebuchadnezzar was astonished; and he rose in haste *and* spoke, saying to his counselors, "Did we not cast three men bound into the midst of the fire?" They answered and said to the king, "True, O king." [25] "Look!" he answered, "I see four men loose, walking in the midst of the fire; and they are not hurt, and the form of the fourth is like the Son of God" (Daniel 3:23-25 – NKJV).**

Just as I was there with Shadrach, Meshach and Abednego in the fiery furnace so many years ago, I am with you always. I will never leave you no matter what trials or hardships you encounter because once you said "yes" to Jesus you became a part of Me. And so, I am committed to bringing you through whatever it may be, unscathed if you let Me. It is My Promise to you. Nothing can separate us but *you*.

When the wind blows, there am I. And with each droplet of rain, so am I. I AM… I AM. Understand My power and know you have access to it all. Love Me, focus on Me, yield to Me.

April 6

I am the great I AM. You only need Me to accomplish My plan. Focus. Focus. There are so many who love Me but insist they are following Me by doing it their own way. Not so. I have said to rest *totally* in Me. That means no worry, no plans except Mine, no nothing except Me. This may sound like you will have no life and will only be doing super spiritual things. But, when you place all in Me – when you put Me first in your life – you will see a richness, a fullness to your life that you never thought possible. And, My guidance will connect you with the right people at the right time in the right place to accomplish My purpose.

I have provided all you need as I am the great I AM. No one, not even you, can do it better than Me. Seek Me in everything. Today… today and forever.

April 7

[2] Consider it pure joy, my brothers and sisters, whenever you face trials of many kinds, [3] because you know that the testing of your faith produces perseverance. [4] Let perseverance finish its work so that you may be mature and complete, not lacking anything (James 1:2-4 – NIV).

Each day you learn a little more and a little more. Look at each situation/circumstance as a learning experience – an experience that draws you closer to Me each day, each moment. Count it all joy that I am teaching you My ways, the ways of the adversary and how you daily overcome. Learn and then rejoice in that learning, for I am at hand... teaching, nudging, pulling and sometimes pushing you to that perfect end.

April 8

Where are you going without Me? Nowhere. Your agenda will not carry you anywhere close to what I have planned for you. You are finite and only know in part. I am infinite and know all with power to fulfill all. If you desire to live up to your full potential – the destiny I have chosen for you – give Me first place now, so I can do the same for you into Eternity. Eternity... forever.

Shadrach, Meshach and Abednego. Remember their example and teach faith in Me with no stops, no qualifications, sharing My Love with mercy. Tell them the life I offer them is all or none. Teach them that there can be no fence-sitting, no middle-of-the-road if they are to experience My kind of faith. Tell them this is My call for them to make necessary changes.

April 9

Whatsoever things you shall ask in My Name, it shall be done. Ask and then turn it over to Me. Let it go. Fret and worry are not acceptable parts of the process. Turn it all over to Me. I know what is before you, more than you do. Trust Me and believe that all things are being handled in My mighty way.

Tell one and all while you rejoice in Me as you rise above your daily challenges. Heed My Word and let My principles guide you in everything you think or do – moment by moment, day by day.

April 10

The meaning of life is too broad for your understanding, but I will reveal what is needed at the right time. Bow in nakedness before Me with a right heart and I will clothe you with My Blood of righteousness, reconciliation and power. It is time for necessary changes and growth.

Unlike this world, selfishness has no place in My Kingdom... only selflessness. Look totally to Me, giving yourself to Me in love, thereby removing self and all the things that accompany it, and yielding/growing to a better you in Christ. You will face challenges, but nothing to fear. I am the Master of all and you are My Heir. There is nothing to fear as you belong to Me and are victorious!

April 11

Never before have I poured out My Spirit as I am doing in these last days. I will use whosoever yields to Me. I am no respecter of persons and I will use any willing vessel/person. Do not look to the so-called big shots to do the greatest works with My Holy Spirit. Look to yourself and others like you, the everyday people. In days of old, I often chose the least likely people to carry My charge. Look at the disciples. They are an example of My desire to use everyone even when they are unlikely candidates. In so doing, others can see what I am able to accomplish to My Glory and it is the same today. I am *no* respecter of persons.

April 12

People must learn of My concern for the little and the big things in their lives, for they are all important to Me. They all fit into a comprehensive plan with one carrying no more weight than the other. They must know/learn that I am the God of *all*. Nothing is too insignificant for My attention and nothing is too large for My control.

Understand that I am the I AM.... Master of all, which means I orchestrate the entire symphony whether it is one syncopated note from the tympani or a flutter of notes from a flute. All parts are important and nothing is too small or too big for

My masterful, loving touch. Without love, yes, I would be untouchable, unreachable. But because I am the God of love, I am concerned about everything that does and does not concern you.

April 13

Now we are ready to move. Things must be done in My time as there is a perfect order. You have mastery of all with Me through faith in Christ Jesus. Trust only in Me.

People change. Things change. But I... I never change. I am always the same – yesterday, today and forever. And, My sameness brings desired change, if you but rely on Me. Let your eyes begin to see nothing else but Me in all situations and watch My peace consume your entire being. Watch how you then become the same through all... like Me.

Peace I bring to you through your faith and trust in Me.

April 14

Walk as I walk... do as I do. Let no man separate you from Me. Greater works will you do as you continue to walk with Me. Match My steps, step by step. I am your protector, your shield, your companion and your miracle worker. Walk with Me and do not allow others to influence you no matter how good their intentions, when you know in your spirit it is not so.

At times, it can be difficult to stand alone when others, especially those you care about, see things in a different way and voice it. But, do not be deterred. As you persevere and are steadfast, many will see the Truth you carry.

April 15

Necessary changes and follow-up are at hand. Some lessons must be learned repeatedly, going deeper layer by layer until you grasp them so firmly they are never forgotten. Share these lessons with Me until they are firmly rooted in you. Then, share them with others.

The spirit world controls the natural world, not the other way around as people would have you believe. Seek first the Kingdom. Always focus spiritually first for your outcomes and the rest shall come to pass naturally.

April 16

Praise be unto Me! I am in control of all situations. *All* situations. Do you think the things that happen in your day-to-day life are a surprise to Me and that anything that happens in this world catches Me off guard? I created the universe, set My plan in motion before the world began and am overseeing it all. Understand that nothing is beyond My control because I am the I AM.

You are not walking alone as I am with you and I will let no evil befall you. You are in control through Me. Know that… not what you feel, but what you know. I am with you. You need nothing else.

April 17

You and Me, together alone.

Spend time with Me – communing with Me, coming to know Me. In whatever circumstance you find yourself, keep the melodies of Me in your heart. Then, you will truly come to know Me. I am the Song of Love and Life that hums through all. Keep your focus on Me and therewith will be our union – your Melody of Life.

Shall we gather at the river – My Living Water that I yearn to share? I offer you life through Me and with Me. What more could you ask? Keep your eyes on Me and praise Me!

April 18

I am the Most High God. As I provide miracles in your life, do not lose sight of how they were brought to you. Never focus on the miracle, for then you have placed an idol, another god, before you. Realize I am the Almighty and have planned to provide you with these riches to use for My Glory today.

Many scholars today say miracles are not for today. Unfortunately, they have not consulted with Me nor deduced the Truth of My miracles. They are for today as they were yesterday and will be tomorrow. To the scoffers I say, "Stop confusing My children with such pronouncements and lessening their faith." But, to you I say, "Do not seek miracles for miracles' sake, but seek their Source – Me."

April 19

You will be able to help many with what I plan for you. Keep self out of the way and remain obedient to My leading. Do not allow the pull of a myopic society cause you to lose sight of the big picture. Do not fall into the cunning traps of the enemy that can pull you into a self-indulgent life. Generosity… giving… blessing people is what we are about and it is most exciting!

Magical moments are at hand. Recognize them and rejoice in them at every opportunity. They are unmatched by anything experienced by you before. Charge on!

April 20

Wonder of wonders I am. Do everything possible in Me not to block the flow of My beauty and joy. Sin is similar to a big cement wall which blocks the flow of traffic if it were placed on a roadway. So it is with Me. I need a clean, clear pathway for My Spirit to flow unobstructed to My proper destination. Forgive yourself for any sins after confessing them to Me, turn from them and we will continue to flow without interruption.

Condemn not yourself, for who better than I to condemn? But, I choose not to as it is not My purpose. I came to draw all men unto Me, not to place more distance between us. If I condemn you not, then why should you? Such is My Love. Partake and see.

April 21

Peace.

Peace I give to you as one of My many gifts. When you are given a gift by a friend, you do not outwardly refuse it or use it for a week then return it. Neither does your friend give you a gift on Monday then ask for it back on Friday. With Me, there is no difference. I give you the gift of Life free of worry and full of peace, and offer My Shoulders to carry all burdens. Sometimes, you do not take it all. But more often, you take it and then give it back to Me. When I told you to neither fret nor worry, I never intended you to apply it periodically. I meant it to apply always. I do not take back My gifts, so do not return them to Me.

Peace I bring to you. Peace I freely and faithfully give to you.

April 22

Faith.

Shadrach, Meshach and Abednego are symbolic of faith in Me and that I am there to walk with you through any fiery place. Keep their example in mind. I can work a miracle out of anything – death, fire, work, health – anything. You need only to look to Me and not allow your circumstances to dictate what is real or what you believe. The Hebrew boys learned to trust Me no matter their situation, and you can, too.

Do you think I change? If I did it then, I can do it now. People change. Philosophies and doctrines change. Seasons change. Times change. But, *I* change not. I am the same yesterday, today and forever.

April 23

Blessed be the Name of the Lord.

My weakness is you – people, My Creation. I have suffered for you and only you... sacrificing My Son, staying with you forty years while you worshipped other gods and showed a total lack of faith in and love for Me, watching while you turned churches into social centers with a watered-down gospel and seeing you choose the Anti-Christ over Me. But, through it all, I have loved you more than you will ever know. And since I know all, I know you will be with Me for Eternity. So, what price My suffering? Very small for what we shall have ad infinitum.

April 24

Glorify My Name in all you do. Patience is one of the hardest lessons, but one which has to be learned to truly reap the rewards of My Kingdom. Patience will move you and your agenda out of the equation and release you to lean on Me and trust the wisdom of My timing. And, it will teach you to endure life's challenges until I say it is time to move on. Many of My disciples, although they love Me, have never learned this lesson. You must for the work ahead.

You are My light in the darkness more than you realize. Continue as you are, stretching to grow through My Word and experience, for the darkness no longer exists where you are.

April 25

Surely the presence of God is in this place!

When I spoke to My people in the hills of the countryside, many were drawn through fascination to hear Me speak or see a miracle. Others came to receive a handout. And, still others came to mock. But, for many who came and were ready to receive, it was simply My Presence that drew them. If I had said nothing and stood in their presence, they would have received all they needed because we were together as one in Spirit.

Today, it is to be the same. As you mature and allow Me to flow through you as My vessel, My Presence in you will minister to the needs of others and draw them to Me. Let others say of you when you are in their midst, "Surely the presence of God is in this place!"

April 26

> **Behold, I give unto you power to tread on serpents and scorpions, and over all the power of the enemy: and nothing shall by any means hurt you (Luke 10:19 – KJV).**

Praise be to Me! I am the Alpha and the Omega. I have power over *all* things and I have given you access to this power through Jesus. Power over all – power to tread on serpents and scorpions, power over sickness and disease, power over poverty, power over the schemes of the enemy. Why do you not use it? It is there for your use. Release My power by faith and use it fully. Then share its use with others. Do not hoard it because it is for all to partake.

April 27

Love never fails (1 Corinthian 13:8a – NIV).

Tantamount to all is loving Me, trusting Me and sharing the Good News. Tasteless evangelism will have to cease and strutting without love can no longer be tolerated. I will remove them or reform them. My Message can no longer be preached/taught without love. Love is what draws people, makes them stay and grow closer… not fear, fire and brimstones. There is no power for your walk in that type of teaching. My Message must be love. From there, people – My people – will want to please Me by following My commandments. *Love never fails.*

April 28

Love through praise.

Loving Me and praising Me are the same in My Eyes. True love for Me puts you in a state of praise and worship. When you love Me with the type of love I seek, you cannot love Me without praising Me. Everything you do should be a form of praise. It should signal to others that you love Me and are exalting Me by your actions.

Praise which comes forth from your mouth is only a small part of real praise. If it is extended without a base in love, it rings hollow to My Ears. Words should be one part of a total you, which can praise Me. Doing all you do with your heart focused on Me is the kind of praise I seek. It is praise that never stops, whether through speech or actions, because your entire being loves Me.

April 29

But my God shall supply all your need according to his riches in glory by Christ Jesus (Philippians 4:19 – KJV).

Where are you going without Me? You are not going forward, but backward. Realize that all movement is for naught without Me. I am the Master Guide and without My direction, there can be no forward movement or progress… it has no lasting importance. But with Me leading and guiding, the gains are everlasting. And, as you learn to hear Me more and more, the clearer becomes My direction. Listen at every point/turn. I am *not* unclear. Hear Me and follow.

April 30

Let your love and joy flow, and do not judge others or gossip about them. It is easy to use your tongue to kill without thinking or speak death unintentionally. But, you *are* your brother's keeper and as such, you are to be a light to others… a strengthener, not a diluter. Keep your eyes on Me and you will see others through My Eyes rather than through your own. Then, love will flow. Exciting!

You want power? You shall have it, but with it comes great responsibility because it must be grounded in My Love. To whom much is given, much is required. So be it. Watch as you and I begin to move as one. I have waited a long time for this moment. Celebration time is here – My celebration and it begins today – *now!*

MAY

May 1

I am the Lord your God. I speak to each one of you in My own clear Voice, specific to you. Do not think you must hear Me in the same way your sister or brother hears Me. I speak to you individually and in a clear way once you know how to listen. Begin to converse with Me and learn the joy of this one-on-one communication.

Certainty of things is not always My way for you. You must walk in faith being certain of just one thing – Me. Know My Promises by knowing My Word.

May 2

> **[9] Wherefore God also hath highly exalted him, and given him a name which is above every name: [10] That at the name of Jesus every knee should bow, of things in heaven, and things in earth, and things under the earth (Philippians 2:9-10 – KJV).**

Many things will be yours through Me. I am the Name above all names and you will use My Name and walk in My power to show others what they are to have.

Once you have fully committed yourself to Me, you will see how My desires become the desires of your heart. Things you felt you would never want or do are often the exact things that I have planned for you. Realize that when you are Mine and walking in maturity, there is no set way I expect you to serve Me. It may be one way today and another tomorrow. Do not decide for Me what way I will use you. Just desire to serve Me in the manner I desire. That is perfection – My desires as yours.

May 3

Sharing, sharing… that is crucial in all types of settings. I have infinite ways to reach My children and it is not until they are mature that they have any awareness of the subtleties at work in their lives. I am in charge of the Master Plan – not to have robotic responses – but I know what you will choose and we are rejoicing here in the knowledge of those choices. Listen to the joy. Joy! Peace! Fellowship! Glory!

Misery is not part of My Kingdom. There is only one who works tirelessly to cause that end, and that is the evil one. Do not confuse his work with Mine. The only thing even distantly connected to Me is when he takes what is Mine and attaches his evil plan to it. I desire only the best for you, and it has been that way since time began. Do not be confused.

May 4

Faith is the almighty tool of My Kingdom. It, along with the Name of Jesus as the basic building block/foundation, are what you need to experience My true Kingdom on earth. You need not wait for physical death to experience the power, joy and peace of life with Me. You have all you need with you now. But, you will not/cannot experience it now or later without Jesus and belief in His Name.

Others will tell you that true Kingdom life will only occur in the sweet by and by when you come to be with Me. But, they fail to understand that I am with you always thereby making the Kingdom not only in you, but around you. Do not be deceived. I am your "right now" Father and have never said the Kingdom was not for today. Will your next life be different from your life on earth? Yes. But, it is all part of the Kingdom stretching into Eternity.

May 5

Never try to second guess, just pray believing that it is done. You do not need to concern yourself with how, for then you begin to set parameters which limit Me. The lovely daisies bloom each year, the trees grow buds/flowers each year even when it appears each winter they are dead. But yet, their beauty unfolds each spring without their/your knowledge of how. How much more can I do with your blooming? Just know that it will happen and enjoy. It is not important for you to know how.

Too often My children forget that while I am their Almighty Father who loves and cares for them, I am also God Almighty – Creator of all. Press to flow in trust and faith that I am in control of everything to its perfect ending/conclusion.

May 6

Majesty.

I am the great I AM. I am the Beginning and the End. I created everything you see before your eyes. But all is for naught without the love of My children. Love and worship are keys to My total happiness – My Love for you, yours for Me, yours for one another. I so want the world to know that I am love in all situations and not as many have told them I am. My saved ones must center themselves on this commandment – love, and let its almighty power flow to everyone, sinners and saved alike. Then all else will come.

Make way for My Love, joy and power. For in truly loving Me you will love others, and the rest will happen as surely as a magnet draws tacks. My way is the only way and should be yours. Once we have reached oneness in your yielding to My complete direction, all of the riches and glory of My Kingdom are yours to be experienced on earth.

May 7

Glory, glory to Me! All of the praise and glory are Mine. And, as a bomb explosion has fall out, so it is through My Glory that blessings will fall out on you – sometimes in a quiet way, other times in an unexpected and explosive way. As long as you keep your eyes on Me, My Hand will be on you in a mighty way.

Doors are opening and you will know which ones to enter and which ones to close. You will know because I will let you know. I am not unclear. I will close what needs to be closed or throw out such a wide invitation you will know you are to enter. Trust Me, for I am not unclear.

May 8

> **And the Word was made flesh, and dwelt among us, (and we beheld his glory, the glory as of the only begotten of the Father), full of grace and truth (John 1:14 – KJV).**

Many will come and many will go, but I desire you to speak My pure, unadulterated Word. I want them to see it spoken through your life. I want them to know what it is for a Christian to live My Word and see My blessings. The Word should be/has been made flesh in all of My children. You should each be a walking Word as My firstborn, Jesus, not Adam. The Word was made flesh and I have given you the power to be My walking Word. Call on this power when you are tired, infirmed, discouraged. My Word made flesh – walking, talking Word – life through My Word, death without it. My Son… My Word… you.

May 9

Majesty of majesties!

Enter My Courts and sup with Me. All that I have is yours. My angels rejoice in your coming and are singing/ringing their praises throughout the heavens. We find joy in the saving of each soul and we celebrate when you learn your place in Me and dine/visit/commune with Me daily. Nothing on earth compares with the loving relationship I have for you.

Come to know Me. Enter My Gates because My Home is yours and we are one. Come and sup with Me. You will not be disappointed. Glory! Hosanna!

May 10

My children must stop crawling and begin to walk. From there, they must learn to run, for how can they do battle if they are crawling on their knees as babies? They must come into the fullness of Me to reach full stature – standing strong and firm, for time is growing short.

Praise be unto Me! I will raise up a people who will go forth boldly – speaking My Word, sharing My Love/joy. I am able to do all things and you are licensed to access all through Me. Use what I offer and do not hold back. Then, you will see the mysteries for so long untold, unfold.

May 11

24 And he cried and said, Father Abraham,
have mercy on me, and send Lazarus, that

he may dip the tip of his finger in water, and cool my tongue; for I am tormented in this flame. [25] But Abraham said, Son, remember that thou in thy lifetime receivedst thy good things, and likewise Lazarus evil things: but now he is comforted, and thou art tormented (Luke 16:24, 25 – KJV).

There is certainty of all with Me and certainty of nothing except eternal damnation without Me. Picture in your mind total separation from Me – the absence of love, joy, peace coupled with excruciating pain, evil, recurring death, darkness – and you will have a taste of what Eternity is when spent with My adversary.

Why would anyone choose him over Me? Much of it is because they do not believe he is real. They do not believe eternal damnation is a reality. They do not believe My Gates exist or know the basic Key to enter is Jesus. They have no understanding of the battle that has been fought and won for them.

They must be told and brought into the fold. They must know what I have done for them and why. They must know what I offer is for everyone. *They must know!*

May 12

He only is my rock, and my salvation; he is my defence; I shall not be greatly moved (Psalm 62:2 – KJV).

Build on Me, for I am the Rock, your Rock. Anything built without My foundation is doomed to fail. Many people picture a house without Me forming the foundation as a house built on sand. But it is much more serious than that. It is likened more to a house built on burning quicksand, all-consuming and never-ending. Eternal death – now and forevermore.

I am the Rock of your foundation and I/you shall not be moved.

May 13

I will build a house – My House – in which My Word will go forth, in which My people will stand on the Rock, My Rock. Double minded, half-stepping can no longer be given a pass. Either you are Mine or you are not. I want a people who choose Me, unequivocally Me. It matters not who, but how… how they come to Me and how they live once they come. I am for everyone and desire not to lose one. Never forget to reach out to others in love, for I am your God of all – the Master Carpenter/Builder constructing with love.

Those who think they will be first may indeed be last. Their choices will make the decision.

May 14

Have I not told you that My Name is above all names? Not just above a few names, but *any* name. Anything you can think of and beyond, My Name is above/higher than it. Internalize this Truth and place it in your heart, so that My adversary can never deceive you. You have been given the authority to use My Name as My Joint Heir. Understand it, use it and stand on it. Do not be deceived, for the greatest battle has already been fought and we have *won!* Hallelujah! Glory! Praise Me!

Stay with Me. Stay with Me. Though you face trials each day, stay with Me. Though it may seem you are at your wit's end and cannot go on, stay with Me because we can conquer all obstacles, all difficulties. And while we are overcoming, you and I, let Me love you and soothe you and give you peace. Let Me smooth your troubled waters. Stay with Me.

May 15

> **And at the ninth hour Jesus cried with a loud voice, saying, Eloi, Eloi, lama sa bach tha ni? which is, being interpreted, My God, my God, why hast thou forsaken me? (Mark 15:34 – KJV).**

"My God, my God, why have you forsaken Me?" I cried. And His answer to Me was, "For My children, that they might live through You." My Father sacrificed Me as an innocent Lamb for the sake of His entire flock. What I suffered was a most abominable thing – separated totally from My Father and carrying sin for all – the entire world – past, present and future. Although it was only for a short while, it seemed an Eternity. But He/I knew He would eventually raise Me up to sit at His Right Hand while all of Heaven rejoiced. That is how much My Father loved/loves you. Know that.

May 16

Glory! Glory! Holy! Holy!

Enter My Gates with thanksgiving and praise. I want to serve My children, but most do not know how to enter My Court. When you ask your mother or father to do something for you, do you just burst into their house or room with no salutation, ask them to do something and expect it to be done? No. You speak first, maybe ask how they are doing, then ask the favor. You know all along they will gladly do what you ask, but you give them the respect of greeting them properly. So it is with Me. I expect you to come to Me in the proper way through My Son, Jesus, and with thanksgiving and praise. I will gladly do anything for you, but I am the Head of the Family and should be approached/respected as such.

May 17

> **3 All things were made by him; and without him was not any thing made that was made. 4 In him was life; and the life was the light of men (John 1:3-4 – KJV).**

Master of all am I. Creator of Heaven and earth. The Designer of the universe. The Architect of life. The Inventor of love/you. Know I am coming soon, and all I have created is/will be at your command – sitting side by side reigning over the universe, the perfect completion of the Ultimate Blueprint.

The world would have you think that all you see is a result of some organized chaos that resulted in the big bang forming creation. Do not let them deceive you, for if there was a big bang, then I was that big bang. Why it is easier for them to believe something as ludicrous as the big bang theory rather than believe I created the universe and beyond is only a deception of the adversary causing man to trust his wisdom rather than Mine. Pray that their eyes will be opened.

May 18

We have much ground to cover, for there is much to learn in a relatively short time period. Do not block new information you receive and prejudge it as wrong. Search My Scriptures. Feed on them and then I, through My Holy Spirit, will give you a clear understanding as to the accuracy of the information. Sometimes I use others in the strangest places to heighten your awareness and give you revelation. Other times, the words coming forth from others are untrue or distorted. You must lean on Me for your understanding by keeping your mind open until *I* show you what is right and proper.

May 19

Total control. I must have total control, not because I want to take over your life, but because you have made a choice to serve Me. Yes, I have the power to control you without your consent, but what kind of love relationship would we share if you were as a robot? That is not what I desire. My desire is in loving Me, you turn all over to My total control, that we may reign together lovingly… victoriously.

It can be frightening to give anyone total control over yourself. But, as you study My Word and spend time with Me in prayer and worship, I will show you there is no one more trustworthy than I. I love you with all My Heart and My utmost intention is to work out My very good plan in your life. Count on it.

May 20

Holy! Holy! Holy! Lord God Almighty!

Confusion is a weapon of the devil. Anytime you find yourself experiencing this, stop whatever you are thinking or feeling and turn it over to Me. Confusion is not of Me, so recognize it immediately – subdue it – and give it release. Remember how I smoothed the waters and stilled the winds for My disciples? Well, the same I do for you. I smooth your troubled waters and I still your turbulent winds. I am peace. I am peace through which comes your calm.

You are body of My Body, flesh of My Flesh and have no less than My best.

May 21

A clandestine love affair with you is not for Me. If you love Me, the time has come for you to shout it from the housetops. How can I confess you to My Father if you cannot speak of Me and show My Love to those around you? Are you ashamed of Me? If not, come out of the closet because you should have nothing to hide. If you do, then let your heart be searched and cleansed... I can do that. Then, take up My banner and go forward. You have nothing to fear and nothing of which to be ashamed.

Come out and go forth with Me. As birds of a feather, My Love, purity and protection shall stick to you like glue.

May 22

For all have sinned, and come short of the glory of God (Romans 3:23 – KJV).

Merciful Father, I am. All of this business about losing your salvation when you slip has got to stop. I am a loving God and know all about you. Do you think I would go through sacrificing My Son to save you, then try to make you lose your salvation? It would not make sense! I want each one of you with Me. I knew of your sin before you were born, but I still saved you. As a Christian, you are not to walk a tightrope in fear of falling off into damnation at any moment. Yes, you were born with a sin nature, but you are My righteousness and are not to walk in fear and anxiety. You are to walk with the joy of Me, knowing you will not always get it right, but because I know your heart, I have designated you as Mine.

Keep your heart right, pure, full of love. Confess your sin and believe it is forgotten, truly forgotten. (Many of you need to forget the wrongs done to you.) Then walk in My light and never fear your loss of salvation, for I love you above all and have planned Eternity with you.

May 23

Lean not to your understanding, but look to Me for all. It is almost beyond My vast comprehension why people find it so hard to lean/depend on the all-powerful I AM. No matter what their accomplishments on their own, they pale against anything they can have with Me. Why they feel what they can see or touch is the most important, can only be due to the interference or distortion of My adversary. Things happen around people each day that they call "luck" or "coincidence" and are satisfied with that. But, when it comes to My spiritual world, walking by faith and not by sight, and understanding I have assigned them power over all things through the Name of Jesus, they think it foreign or impossible.

My charge to you is to take My Love which permeates My entire plan, couple it with belief/trust in Me and My Word, and walk in the power given you before time began. This is not a time for babies who know all of the songs about Jesus and can quote a few well-known Scriptures. This is a time of growing up and speaking out. This is a time of warfare when it is necessary for you to lean on Me and not to your own understanding.

May 24

The Power is in Me.

The power is in Me, and I have assigned it to you as My Joint Heir. I have written My will, if you will, and have named you benefactor of everything I have. Therefore, take it. The will (Word) has been written and states that you may receive all that is in it. So then, do you just take part of it for now and save the rest for later? No. My will has been prepared and given to you. You have inherited everything, everything in it. Therefore, take it, use it and live as a true heir of the mightiest Kingdom.

This is a time when you must know what you have in Me without question, so you may go forth boldly. My Promises are for now not later, and I am bound to keep them. Stand on them, believe in them, take them for My greater Glory.

May 25

When I call, answer and then act as you are directed. That is true obedience to Me. I should be so ingrained in your spirit a nudge/ruffle in your spirit may serve as My Call, or a thought flashing through your mind might be My Call. Then your immediate response – so subtle you do not recognize it until you look back. That is what our relationship is to be. My Spirit so much a part of you, there is no prior thought of your distinguishable response to Me. It is a flowing, back and forth... back and forth, as we move as *one*.

May 26

People make things so difficult for themselves when they could just lean on Me for all of their answers, all of their cares. What is in them? The desire to do it their way and make their own decisions is where the difficulty lies. But, it also makes them more precious to Me. More precious because I know when they finally make that commitment to serve Me, they have made the all-important choice not as programmed robots but as free-thinking beings. They have decided to put themselves aside and to lean on Me. Then I can begin to work with them.

Unfortunately, most people have not learned what it means to fully lean on Me. Show them each day and in every way the joy of My undying support.

May 27

Rest in Me.

Rest in Me, your Majesty of Majesties. All things are at your feet already conquered, if you but rest in Me. All things have been planned for your good, if you but rest in Me. There is no detail too large or too small that I am not aware of and for which I have not made plans. Remember that I know all, see all and am all – that I existed before time and will exist through all Eternity. Realizing My Omnipotence/Omniscience, why would you not rest in Me, the all-seeing I? Begin to meditate on Who I am and the relationship you have with Me. Then rest in Me.

Many do not know what true rest is. It means you turn all over to Me without fear or anxiety. It means you take each day at a time, unmoving, until My guidance is clear. Rest means letting Me handle all of your problems and cares although not in the sense of laziness or disinterest, but knowing I am caring for you and showing you what to do and when to do it. You then move at that time and in that manner with a peace only I can provide. That is My Rest.

May 28

Miracles are for today. So many preachers teach that My miracles are not for today and they must be told/shown they are wrong. I have given you the authority to perform miracles, to walk in My power. Miracles should be occurring in My Body/ Church on such a regular basis they are considered almost commonplace. I say "almost" because the Source should never be forgotten. The power in a Christian's life should be evident at all times whether facing a particular circumstance, laying hands on the sick, casting out demons or walking in love and joy. Your life should be a total manifestation of My miracle-working power in these last days. Therefore, know your authority in Me and exercise it daily knowing that it is My will. Miracles are for today – let no one tell you otherwise.

Mission work is not necessarily done on some foreign soil or even in a ghetto of a large city. Mission work should be done in the home, at work, on the street, in the grocery store. Your entire being should be permeated with a desire to provide service as My disciple wherever you are. It should never deter or detract from the setting but be an extension of it, meaning you allow Me to use you in the perfect way. When you force your discipleship, the result will be disruption, confusion, rejection. But, when you follow My lead, all will be in the perfect time, in the perfect way.

May 29

Praise be to Me! I am the Rock of your salvation – never changing, your solid Rock. Realize what this means. A rock is solid. It is not like sand or marsh or dirt. It is firm and strong. Do not let others tell you your salvation is not built on My Rock. Do not let them make you think you have to walk a tightrope, scared your Rock/salvation will crumble. There is certainty in Me and there is freedom in Me. Do not be misled by those who have no real understanding of what I am as your Rock. From this foundation springs My House, My Temple, the new you. And together we dwell as one, loving one another as we conquer all.

Why would My Father allow Me to suffer as He did and then place Me at His Right Hand, if He did not want to save you and cleanse you of your sins? He would not. Think about what you have in Me and know it is solid and forever.

May 30

I am your champion. As the knight of old fought for the hand of his damsel, so I do for you. I have fought all battles, conquered the dragon/Satan for the hand of My Bride – you/the Church – and now await the Day when we reign together as one in My Kingdom. But for now, know My Love for you knows no bounds and I have gone before you in all battles to clear the way. Know I am your Knight in shining armor and await your heart.

The warfare of which I speak is spiritual and more far-reaching than anything fought on an earthly plane no matter how devastating.

May 31

As the squirrel stores nuts away for the winter, store Me in your heart for your "winters."

My people have the notion that it is normal to react to difficult circumstances such as death and sickness as the world does. They have no more understanding of what is normal than a baby understands night and day. What is normal for those outside of Me should not be the same for My Body. With each situation there should be rejoicing, knowing there has been triumph. Not easy? Not easy on your own, but certainly no problem with Me. *Count it all joy... in whatsoever circumstances... therewith to be content.* These lessons must be learned or your life will never be victorious. Joy in all things. My joy through your being.

Store Me in your heart for your "winters." Dwell on this as I dwell in you.

JUNE

June 1

I am well pleased with you, but there is so much more to do. To grow in Me and come to know Me is of great importance. But, spreading your knowledge of Me must be tantamount. I urge you to bring the lost to Me rather than sit comfortably in the knowledge of Me as many do. Take Me first within you, and then to the world.

Why should I tell you all of this… only to keep to yourself? No. I desire that you receive it in your innermost being, your spirit, and share it with all. Each disciple has this charge: to go forth with My Word, not in any one set way, but in all ways and in all situations. I am to be present at every turn. Therefore, keep Me in your remembrance.

June 2

One day they will all believe me – you will see. One day they will all believe Me when they see I am the Key. One

day they will all believe Me when they are set free. One day they will all believe Me and they will praise Me!

What is your life without Me? Nothing. People often think they have it made. They have houses, money, cars, good jobs, friends. But, they have nothing. The things of this world are short-lived and meaningless in the total scheme of things. None of it can be brought with them when they die. None of it can provide salvation. None of it offers eternal life. The "things" you place importance on today are worth nothing tomorrow.

Understand that through Me you have the best of everything at your fingertips. You are royalty and reign victoriously with Me forevermore. Do you understand what that means? In this life, it means joyfully and lovingly controlling and not reacting to circumstances. And upon death – physical death – Life Eternal as My Joint Heir.

June 3

Before time began, I have always had you in mind. Nothing in your life is by chance. It has been planned since the beginning of time. And, you are more important to Me than you will ever know. Yes, you have some idea from the gifts I have granted to you. But, to know all this has been planned for you and Me to be together for all time, is more than you can truly grasp. Think about a world, earth before Creation… empty, void, non-existent… and know My thoughts were of you even then.

June 4

He that hath ears to hear, let him hear (Matthew 11:15 – KJV).

When I speak, listen in the best way you know how. I do not expect you to be able to hear Me in any way different than where you are, where I have brought you presently. I do not expect you to hear Me in the same way someone else might hear Me or even to respond as another is led to respond. But, I do expect you to have your ears tuned to Me constantly and act according to your level of spiritual maturity. You are never judged or compared to anyone else. I have My own measuring stick and you are expected only to do what I am teaching *you* to do and no one else.

Too often you place your eyes on others and think, "Well, he is doing thus and such and she is doing that." However, with all they might be doing, you have no way of knowing about their obedience to Me, nor should you. No. Listen with your inner ear/the Holy Spirit and believe I have designed your special lesson for that time – totally individual, totally unique. Then, comes obedience… listening and responding until I bring you to your next understanding, thereby stretching you to My Glory.

June 5

Seldom have My children stopped to consider the magnitude of their existence/creation. That I created the entire universe – the stars, the water, the earth, chose them to inhabit earth as heirs and offer them life eternal with Me – is thought of in such a casual manner. It would be amazing, if I did not already know it would be so. It is time for all to recognize Me – to recognize Me in everything, to realize I am everything and realize who they are in Me. It is time for the Body to wake up and know Me and My ways, then grow into the fullness that has been prepared for them.

We have much to do, but your direction is clear. Tell them of Me and My Love.

June 6

Sharing one with another.

When you have given all you can give, know I am there to refill you and refresh you… to bring you to another level of fullness. In My Kingdom, your supply shall never be exhausted – there is always more. Therefore, is it not easier and more sensible to look to Me for your provision? I have told you I will not give you more than you can bear. So, there is no need to rely on your own understanding. It is as if you were going to your piggy bank when you have access to the riches of the universe. It makes no sense. Remove self and rely on Me for your all as a child relies on his parents – without hesitation, without thought.

You are My *Love-child* – created by love/God, with love, for love. My Love for you knows no bounds. It is limitless, never ending, never changing. You are My Love manifested and made complete. Let each part of you reflect that love. Let each part of you demonstrate My Love within you and show the true meaning of love as My *Love-child*.

June 7

My power is within you always. Consider Me first and not your surroundings. You have missed many of My blessings because you doubt in the smallest recesses of your heart. It matters not what you have been taught in the past or what you see. To believe fully and have no doubt is a fullness of faith confessed at each point. Erase the natural circumstances by your spirit-talk, your spirit-walk, your spirit-faith... and all doubt will flee.

In this last day, we must have armies of power-believers for the work which is at hand. I call you as a *faith-walker* to go forth by My Spirit in My power!

June 8

> **...but to think soberly, according as God hath dealt to every man the measure of faith (Romans 12:3 – KJV).**

To every man, I have given a measure of faith. Use it and commit yourself to making it grow each day. Do you not have faith that you will wake up each day? Do you not have faith that you will continue breathing as you should? So, as your Creator, why not faith in Me? Faith that is such a part of you gives no thought to its working, its operation. It simply is and does not have to be worked up or imitated. It is this level of faith that releases My Promises and sends forth My power. It is your undying faith manifested which seats you fully in My Courts – faith to believe My Love for you, faith to believe My sacrifice for you, faith to walk in My authority. Rejoice! I am not asking more of you than you can do. I never do.

June 9

Keep the smile of Me in your heart at all times. It matters not what circumstances you face – death, disease – My joy must flow through you as surely as the sun rises each morning. When you have reached that point, you have at last come to know Me... knowing My Love and joy course through all. It is this level I seek for you, that you may know Me more each day.

My celebration with you is better than the finest food or wine. Whatever you fancy as the most outstanding experience for you, I am better. Whether it is the joy of being given a million dollars, I am better. Whether it is being the best there is in your particular field of endeavor, I am better. No matter what you value as the most exciting, the epitome of all, I am better. I am the best and through Me you become the best. Never doubt Me or your place with Me, for I am all you need.

June 10

> **"Look at the birds of the air; they do not sow or reap or store away in barns, and yet your heavenly Father feeds them. Are you not**

much more valuable than they?" (Matthew 6:26 – NIV).

As the birds chirp outside your window in the morning, know I am there. See how I have created and cared for them? Did I not tell you how much more I would care for you? I have equipped them to have food, protection – to survive. In a greater manner, I have equipped you to not only survive, but to be victorious. Look at the creatures around you and marvel at the wonder of My care for them. Then, realize that you, as My child, are cared for in a greater way through My Word. Begin to take this time to absorb the beauty of Creation, so you may know what you are in Me.

June 11

A railroad train toots loudly as it approaches a sleepy little town to let everyone know it is nearing time to get on board. Not so with Me. Yes, the trumpets will sound and fill the heavens to announce My coming, but with My train, you will not have time to make any last-minute arrangements. If you have been prepared for My return/have your bags packed, then you will hear My whistle and be ready to board with Me. But, if you have not accepted Me because you thought you had so much time or it was just a bunch of nonsense, then you are liable to miss My train. Pack your bags... pack your bags with Me and get ready to board My Heaven-bound train.

Sentimental journeys with Me may fill you outwardly and inwardly. But, in your journey with Me, outward feelings must never dominate. Emotions can run high, but they are as seed falling on cement if they are not rooted spiritually. Journey with Me and let your innermost part flow.

June 12

Singly I came. Singly I saved. Freely I came. Freely I gave.

It is time for the world to wake up and realize the dynamics of what I have done for them and what I am still doing, for that matter. I came to save, not because I was forced to, but because I am love. Through Me, all was given to you freely with love. But, Mine is a love that many cannot grasp. They are not attached to Me and question how it can be. How can so much come freely with love?

Understand what you have in Me and that all was planned for your understanding. Then, tell them and show them what I have done.

June 13

> **For now we see in a mirror, dimly, but then face to face. Now I know in part, but then I shall know just as I also am known (1 Corinthians 13:12 – NKJV).**

Moonlight shining across the night water, safely guides boats along their way. The moon is but a reflection of the sun, but it illuminates the darkness in a magnificent way. The light you see from Me is much the same in that you are seeing a reflection of Me. Even so, from this lighted reflection, this glass darkly, I am able to light the world. I reflect to you, you reflect to others and they in turn reflect My light to someone else. Imagine the fullness of My light, face to face, when we sit together through Eternity.

Watch My light as it grows more and more each day in you.

June 14

Watching and waiting... watching and waiting.

In your life with Me, learn to have the patience to wait on Me. You cannot fully serve Me without it – watching each little incident and knowing it is never a coincidence, waiting for Me to show you what your role is in a situation, watching for My Presence in whatever you see, hear or do and waiting for My return. Although it may seem as time wasted, it is during this time when I will mold you and make you into who I have designed you to be – perfect and complete. And, understand that Mine is a relationship that grows daily with your watching and waiting... watching and waiting.

June 15

Thou shalt have no other gods before me (Exodus 20:3 – KJV).

As we draw nearer to My return, realize that Satan has pulled out all of the stops and is making a mighty effort to lure you from Me. Know that he is desperate because his time is coming to a close. Beware of his tricks and deal with him accordingly, for you know we have the upper hand. Do not take a noncommittal attitude, for it is not time to slumber and sleep. I did not create you to be in the dark. No! I created you to be in the light, My light. So, be alert and ready to call him the liar he is. Know that I am your only God and we are drawing closer to our purest time together. Oh, how I await that day!

June 16

It is as you have known – I never send sickness, poverty or anything like it. Over the years, I have taken the blame for so much evil of My adversary. And, because of the misconceptions, it has kept many of My children babies, attributing wrongdoing to Me. I am perfection and all I have created is perfection. I could no more create evil and sickness than you could understand My Word without My Spirit. The time has come when a fuller understanding of Me and My ways must go forth. It has been told wrong for too long. You have your charge and it must be done. Time is growing short and in these last days, they need to know Me in My fullness to accomplish the tasks at hand.

June 17

Time is growing short.

The Body, My Body must begin to move in its appointed way to reach the lost. It matters not that you have never reached out in like manner or you are not sure what your function is. I, your God, can handle all of that. You walk in faith – I lead and guide you. You do not need to know or have experience when it comes to Me, for My Holy Spirit can and will show you what to do and say. Lean on Me. Rest in Me. Walk in faith. The unknown may cause fear in you, but I am not fear. Therefore, to walk with Me is to walk with Me in faith, peace and love. Be ready for My direction and follow, for I will use any person who wills it. Time is growing short.

June 18

Singly you can do nothing, but together we can do all. Understand your strength, even your existence is in Me. When you face different trials or temptations, never think even for a moment that you are alone. Realize I dwell in you and have given you access to all through My Name. Know we walk together under My direction, shoulder to shoulder, able to meet and conquer any circumstance, for I am in you and you are in Me. We are one… never alone.

Elements of joy are in everything. You need to look, however, sometimes with a microscopic eye to determine it. As I am Creator of all purity and joy, find Me in your bleakest hour. There is nothing you may encounter for which I cannot provide My joy. Joy is My gift to you, and as Me, it is never changing. I am always joy.

June 19

Nehemiah said, "Go and enjoy choice food and sweet drinks, and send some to those who have nothing prepared. This day is holy to our Lord. Do not grieve, for the joy of the Lord is your strength" (Nehemiah 8:10 – NIV).

I am your joy. I am your strength. My joy is your strength. Long-faced Christians display a reversed image of what I am. It is no wonder the world is so confused about why anyone would want to be a Christian. Who wants to come into something that appears so bleak and forlorn with so many do's and don'ts? No, they must see My joy in you. They must see how you daily overcome in joy. The light of your joy coupled with your beacon of love is what makes Me irresistible to the world. Recognize My joy, receive it and as it flows through your life, let it bubble over to those outside. I am your joy and indeed your strength. Let your entire being speak joy. *Joy!*

June 20

Necessary/essential steps and changes.

As you keep your eye on Me, be aware that each occurrence, each experience is not by happenstance. Realize there is something to be drawn from your circumstance that brings you closer to Me. Learn the lessons thoroughly, so that when My adversary attacks, you will know your strength in Me and will automatically switch your gears into overdrive.

I know you love Me. But, without the daily lessons in the knowledge of Me, you have not the power to overcome. Meet each encounter with joy knowing it is yet another time of experiencing the Jewels of your inheritance in growing and knowing Me.

June 21

> **If we confess our sins, he is faithful and just and will forgive us our sins and purify us from all unrighteousness (1 John 1:9 — NIV).**

Mercy to one and all! I am your merciful Father. I knew all you would do/would choose before time began. I knew the mistakes you would make and then ask forgiveness for. I knew it all and yet I chose you. My children must understand this! They must understand that I cover them with the Blood of My Son, and they need only make their confession to Me with a truly repentant heart and they are forgiven. Separation from you is not My aim. I have made it so easy for all to be with Me yet for millenniums, people have tried to make it harder or simply have made it harder through their own lack of knowledge.

I am your merciful Father and await your confession.

June 22

The awakening of My Spirit in the Church while the world is at the same time becoming more carnal and base is merely a sign of the times. Did I not tell you it would be so? My Word does not change… it does not lie. However, most do not even look to the Holy Scriptures or to Me to know what is to be. Others are surprised when a natural phenomenon occurs which fulfills/confirms My Word. But, My Word will always be verified, for I know all. Oh! If only they would look to Me. Now, it behooves you to look to Me for your answers. Know you are in the last days before My return and what you see are merely signs of the times.

June 23

Blessed assurance, Jesus is mine.

Know always that I am with you. Know always that I will never leave you nor forsake you, for did I not tell you so? My purpose for you is that we shall never be separated, that is, in this life or the next. My plan for you is that each day you know Me better as we grow into oneness. My desire is for all the world to know My Love transcends all… and in loving you so greatly, I cannot bear the loss of even one. I am with you every moment awaiting your awareness of My Presence, awaiting our glorious time together. I have never planned to leave you because in growth to oneness, how could it be so? It would be impossible.

June 24

Natural affection, one for another, should never be confused with spiritual love. Spiritual love, My Love, is the purest form. Once My Love is deeply rooted in you, it will flow in a natural way – automatically, without distinguishing one person from another.

It is non-discriminating love, freely given as I have given to you. My Love is what *I* seek for all to have and to share. When you experience it as one of My Love-creatures, you cannot help but pass it along – it simply flows without any thought from you. So many are without love of any kind. I desire that you show them the love that can be theirs in My Family – love on the highest plane.

June 25

> **11 ...behold, the LORD passed by, and a great and strong wind rent the mountains, and brake in pieces the rocks before the LORD; but the LORD was not in the wind: and after the wind an earthquake; but the LORD was not in the earthquake:**
> **12 And after the earthquake a fire; but the LORD was not in the fire: and after the fire a still small voice (1 Kings 19:11-12 – KJV).**

When I speak, listen. Listen for My Voice as I give direction. Often, My Voice is heard in a clear, firm way – full and bold. But most often, it is evidenced as a still small Voice. Many times, My Voice is missed because you are looking for Me to come in a certain way and I come in another way. Expect to hear Me in different ways, thereby leaving the door open for

My clearest guidance. Expect always to hear Me speak, but without your limitations. Determine in your heart to listen and know I am always there communicating with you in My perfect way.

June 26

Come before the Mercy Seat and receive your forgiveness. Wallow not in your pity of self. Come before Me for your forgiveness. Think on this – a God of love such as I, wants His children joyful and happy, not running around with sadness and condemnation in their hearts.

A god is thought to be able to do things beyond mortal man because he is a god. But, I am the God of love, the God of all gods, and *can* do anything. Therefore, do you think I would not make a way for you to be cleansed and joyful? Do you think I would not plan a way out of all situations since I know all things? Understand that I, as your God of love, am also merciful and all-knowing and expect you to be joyful. How can you reign with your head hung down? Bring yourself before Me to receive the cleansing which was already assigned to you, and know what it is to be a true child of God.

June 27

Marriage should be to Me first, then to one another. Oh, how I await the day when I can fully receive My Bride, the Church. Such rejoicing as never before! It is for this very reason it is time for My Body to ready itself for Me, to be ready, for you know not when I will return. My Bride must be pure and spotless. Therefore, a purging is now beginning to cleanse the Church of its illiteracy of Me as well as its unscriptural teachings. The time is now for old, childish things to be put away and for the Church to grow up in Me. It is time to get ready!

June 28

When the Spirit is mixed with self, depending on the portions of each, they will determine the final potion – like flour and sugar in batter or vinegar and oil. I am always clear, but whenever My Messages/directions go through your vessels there are liable to be varying degrees of distortion. As you become more like Me, the distortion decreases because you serve as a pathway/channel rather than an interpreter. The less your natural self is involved the greater the clarity.

Strive to let My Spirit increase in you while lessening your natural self. The result will be astounding – a growing together of you and Me into oneness, without obstacles, without barriers.

June 29

Shelter yourself from all adversity in Me. As your home shelters you from all unfavorable weather conditions – the wind, the rain, the cold, the heat – so can I shelter you. But, I do so much more. Through Me, your Fortress, you can protect yourself from anything which comes against you spiritually and physically – any plots and plans of the enemy or his fiery darts. My Name is above all. Use it. Use Me. I am your shelter in any condition, any circumstance, and long to protect and secure you one and all.

My Body must come to know what they have in Me to do the work which is at hand. Understand first, then share your understanding with them.

June 30

You know what you know and must never let anyone/anything convince you otherwise. So often when you are almost to the point of seeing a much-desired outcome manifest, everything appears to the contrary. Most often, it is My adversary attempting to discourage you so you are robbed of My Promises. It is at that time, especially at that time, when you should get with Me in your prayer closet and pray constantly while you stand on My Word.

Place your eyes totally on Me and not on your surroundings, for they will not tell you the truth. Do not allow yourself to waver to the right or the left regardless of your circumstances. Be steadfast and immovable because it is then and only then, you know what you know is so.

JULY

July 1

I am the best Friend anyone could ever have and most do not even know Me. I am always there, loving and caring for you, waiting to do you a service. I love you when you turn your back on Me. I love you when your teeth are not brushed and your hair is not combed. I love you when you have "feel sorry for yourself" days. I love you when you show no love, when you are uncharitable.

I love you always and desire only as you draw nearer to Me, you love Me and share My Love with others. Of whom else could you say the same? I am your All. I am your Friend.

July 2

> **And they that went before, and they that followed, cried, saying, Hosanna; Blessed is he that cometh in the name of the Lord (Mark 11:9 – KJV).**

I was sent for you. I was sent to do My Father's work here on earth. Having completed that part, I sit now at the Right Hand of My Father with love for you. Your part now is to carry on My Father's work and take the Good News/the Gospel to the world, but not without Me. You have Me to lead and guide you as we make this journey together. You have Me to intercede for you with My Father. You have Me for any and all of your needs. Know your trip has been painstakingly planned and you have first-class arrangements.

Reverence and honor are due Me. Stand on My Promises believing they are done. It is as though you call Me a liar when you know My Promises and do not take them at face value or act upon them. I am not a liar. I am Truth of the purest form. Honor Me by honoring My Legacy to you.

July 3

> **Trust in the Lord with all thine heart; and lean not unto thine own understanding (Proverbs 3:5 – KJV).**

Wisdom of the highest form is what I have for you. I am the Reservoir… and all you need do is tap into Me for the wisdom needed for everyday and spiritual matters. Lean not to your own understanding. My Word, My Spirit – they are all you need with your willingness to follow. You need never have confusion or despair, for I am there to answer your questions and supply your needs. With wisdom such as Mine at your very fingertips, why would you not use it? I am the all-seeing, all-knowing I. What I have I give to you in love. Use it.

July 4

Shamefully they/My disciples hid while I was taken off to be crucified. But did I stop loving them? No. They were doing the best they could for what they understood. As you recall, I came back to them. And, so it is with you. I expect only the best that you can do for your maturity level at the time. Another time, I expect more because you know more. But I never, never stop loving you no matter what your outcome.

Stretch yourself to reach the limitless I AM. There are no limits in Me except those placed there by you. Now is the time for all My children to reach, to expand into the fullness of Me because there is so much more that I have freely given to you. As you go through each circumstance, know I am bringing you forward, stretching you to a new understanding that leaves you much further ahead. Believe you are limitless in Me and let us rise to new heights *together.*

July 5

Dear one, never ever think I cannot handle all. Never ever think what you ask in My Name is too small. Never ever think your request is too bizarre when you are seeking My perfect will. Ask and it shall be done as I am God of all, with power to do anything for you. Ask believing, and it shall be done. It is

My purpose for it to be so and there is no room for doubt and unbelief in your walk with Me.

Never fret or worry. They are not of Me. Remember that. I am peace and I am love. There is nothing which can come against you that I cannot neutralize if you but ask. Ask, and believe it done/see it done in Me.

July 6

On Christ the solid Rock I stand, all other ground is sinking sand.

Let Me be your Rock, not only for salvation, but for everything. Let Me be your stability, for I am ever-present and never changing. In this world of constant shifts – changing philosophies and ideas – I am the Rock upon which all should stand. I am the Foundation without which nothing should be built. I am your solid Rock which has stood/is standing/will stand the test of time.

Others may promise to be there for you and sincerely mean it, but there is no one other than Me that can guarantee it. No matter how the world spins around you with its negative situations and influences, I am your firm foundation upon which you can stand and stand and stand. Never forget that your feet are planted on solid ground and that ground, that foundation is Me.

July 7

The sanctity of My Church must be foremost. I must have a Body which is pure of heart, which has put away the things of the world and is serious about Me... serious about its relationship with Me. You are My Bride. What husband will accept a bride who is not serious about her union with him? What wife comes to her husband in a soiled wedding dress? As clearly as you see the spotted gown, I see the spotted heart. The time is now for My Bride to be cleansed so she may greet Me spotlessly.

Confess what has spotted you, repent – make up your mind to turn away from it – and love Me. I await you with an open Heart and open Arms.

July 8

Love must be first. A clearer understanding of the depth of My Love for you is necessary before you can even consider walking in My power and experiencing My Promises. When you understand My Love, then you will understand My Promises. Not why or how they work, but because of My Love for you they *do* work. Next, as an outgrowth of our love relationship comes faith. Faith – that because I love you so, in giving your heart to Me, it is as I have said. I have given all to you to walk in My power while on earth, to dwell in My Kingdom now rather than upon physical death. First love... then faith... then the power of My Kingdom Promises.

July 9

Always be aware that as I am ever-present, so too, is My adversary and his legion of liars. You must know that, so you are ready at every turn to see through him and his antics, and combat him victoriously. Many do not even consider him real. But he is real – not to be feared, but to know he is always there trying to pick and pull you away from Me and My plan for you. Never let him do this.

Know we together have power over him, for I have no plan to lose you. Know we are victorious, and have been since the beginning of time.

July 10

Faith is the all-important key for releasing My Love and power. My Body will have to grow in its level of faith to a point of believing I can do all things, I am in control of everything and I work all to good. Faith is My Lesson, for without it you can never please Me or know the quality of My Love for you or experience My Omnipotence/power.

I never had in mind a crippled Church, weak and ineffective. But, without a continually growing belief in Me, you are crippled. Cast your doubts aside and use Me as your only crutch, your stability. My Church was meant to stand tall and to walk erect in power through faith in Me. Understand what you have in Me through faith.

July 11

Wonder and awe are due Me although you will never entirely know the enormity/vastness of Me. However, you may come to know Me more each day, each hour, each minute, each second, as that is what I desire for you... that you may come to know

Me more intimately. Wonder encourages you to hunger and seek like the innocence of a child searching for answers, which I adore, whereas doubt only separates you from Me. Desire in your innermost self that your hunger for knowledge of Me increases and I will feed that hunger. Come, let us sup as one.

July 12

Transmission of My Word throughout every part of your being is what I desire for you – not Me for certain situations and you/your sinful nature for others. I need to be in each part of you to manifest My plan for you, a plan laid out before I set time in motion. Feed on Me until you have no choice but to meet each encounter as I would. Commune with Me constantly, so you do not even perceptibly ask, "What would Jesus do here?"

I am speaking of a fuller knowledge and understanding of Me. Strive for My revelations and they shall be yours. Then allow, even encourage them to overflow to everyone you meet.

July 13

> **"To him the doorkeeper opens, and the sheep hear his voice; and he calls his own sheep by name and leads them out" (John 10:3 – NKJV).**

When I speak, listen and know My Voice – learn how to discern My Voice, My leading. How do you do this? By daily seeking Me in My Word by My Holy Spirit. And, when you finally recognize Me, finally know... no one but no one, can tell you it is not I. Know Me. Know My Voice, for there is much to learn, much to discuss. Over the years, I have often spoken to you and you have not heard. I say this not to condemn, but so you will know how much I long for our communication, our sharing. Let this be the beginning of something new and deeper between you and Me. *I love you so much!*

July 14

Totally involved.

I am the Lord your God. But more importantly, I am Abba Father. I am with you at each moment loving you as only I can, making certain all goes according to My plan. I am your guide. I am your shield. I am your shelter. I am your strength. I am your peace. I am your love. I am your righteousness. I am your *everything* from beginning to end and all in between. Think of Me as totally involved, for I am your *all*... totally committed, totally involved. I will never leave you nor forsake you – *not ever*.

July 15

Keep the eyes of your heart on Me for that is what holds the greatest importance. Outward displays of affection are not what I seek. What lies in the heart is what reaches Me – what you are saying and thinking of Me when only I can see. The purity of the heart is what brings Me the greatest joy.

I know all and see all, so you cannot hide from Me what you do not want seen. So, allow My Holy Spirit to shine the spotlight of Truth on your heart and cleanse it once and for all. I desire that you would be made whole in purity, truth and love.

July 16

Shallowly relating to Me cheats you of what you truly have in Me. Yes, you can be content with a simple love for Me. But you cannot experience My fullest joy without a broader, more intimate knowledge of Me. You cannot understand just how much I love you if you do not strive to learn of Me.

My power which is placed in trust for you lies dormant when you allow yourself to stagnate without growth. But, as you seek Me in all things while you strive to know Me, you will know how much I love you and experience more of Me.

So many use Me as a plaything… pulling Me out of the so-called toy chest at their convenience and shutting Me away when they care not to be bothered. I am not to be toyed with. Either you have Me in your life or not – there is no room for the *in-between*. I am either as I have said I am, or I am not. You make the decision as I leave it to you. Once you have chosen Me, then all decisions should be left to Me.

July 17

> **Give, and it shall be given unto you; good measure, pressed down, and shaken together, and running over… (Luke 6:38 – KJV).**

Sharing one with another is My Call to you. Many only think of this verse in terms of giving money or material things, but I am calling you to share – My Love, your love, yourself. Love and compassion have been blatantly omitted in much of My Body. Letting My Love flow one to another is the only way to draw others to Me. But, it is not simply saying it, it is doing it – manifesting My Love in you which means walking in love and talking love. Receive My Love and release its flow to all you meet. As you give it, much more will be given to you. *Love.*

July 18

> **14 And this is the confidence that we have in**
> **him, that, if we ask any thing according to**
> **his will, he heareth us: 15 And if we know that**
> **he hear us, whatsoever we ask, we know that**
> **we have the petitions that we desired of him**
> **(1 John 5:14-15 – KJV).**

I give gladly all I have to you. Come…partake. It is yours for the asking. Ask and you shall receive. You have not because you ask not or you ask amiss. I await your request. Notice I did not say requests, but request.

When you ask believing, you need not continue to ask repeatedly, for you should know it is done. If you have not the belief/faith to know your request has been answered, then ask until that belief is deep down inside of you. What you must do constantly is thank Me for what I have done, am doing and will do. Praise Me unceasingly, but you need not nag Me for your answer to a particular prayer. Your faith and confession are what must be constant and unwavering, not the repetition of your prayer.

July 19

> **Keep back thy servant also from presumptuous *sins*; let them not have dominion over me (Psalm 19:13 – KJV).**

I do not need anyone to provide My answers for Me, not even you. Often you have come up with your own answer as though I had given it to you and you have suffered as a result. That is not what I want. I take no pleasure in seeing you suffer. It is as I have said. Listen for My response. Your impatience for a conclusion will not move Me, for you will always have your answers and they will always be given at the perfect time, in My perfect way. Do not fill in for Me, as I know all and can handle all. Listen and believe you have received My perfect response at My appointed time.

July 20

Many will come and many will go, but My Love is forever. And, what I seek are those of My Body who will love Me as soundly and as steadily as is possible in their earthly bodies. It is a time of weeding out the unsound from the sound – those who would have you believe they are a rock in Me, but they are not. For the work to be done as I have planned, I must have workers who are grounded in My Word, filled with My Love, and ready to serve in obedience. I must have obedience, for how can you serve Me as I desire if after all is said and done, you are not yielding to My will and direction? Decide who you will serve. Once this decision is made, along with your obedience and love for Me, we can truly move together in the world.

July 21

Sharing My Word with others is what I call you to do. That Jesus died for you as a Lamb at slaughter must be realized, but not with simple emotionalism that so many display. It must be reflected upon and the depth of it understood in your spirit. Not simply what happened physically, but what He/We gave up and suffered to walk in this realm, all for your ultimate good. When you genuinely think of what He/We did for you, you can no longer question My Existence, My Love, My power. Spend time dwelling in Me until you have reached your better understanding. Then, take it to the world.

July 22

> **...choose you this day whom ye will serve... but as for me and my house, we will serve the Lord (Joshua 24:15 – KJV).**

My Kingdom is one based in service. You serve as you are served. The greater your service to Me, the more I am able to serve you. Think of Me bowing and washing My disciples' feet even knowing they would betray Me. Just as I did, learn to humble yourself and have no objection to performing the lowliest task, to do what I expect of you in My Kingdom. I am not speaking of works that seem to preoccupy so many brothers and sisters... works they feel are for Me but are, in actuality, for themselves. No, I am speaking of a yielding, a removal of self which is replaced with a yearning to do the simplest task. When you have reached this point, then you are ready to provide the greatest service. It is then the last become first and the first, last. Praise God!

July 23

Shed no tears when you reflect on the times you have not acted Christ-like or even when you doubted My very existence before you accepted Me by faith. Be thankful that God, as the Master Planner, knew all and still chose you to belong to Him. Give praise that through your simple repentant confession, everything of the past is forgiven. Shout hallelujah that we start each day afresh with the covering of My Blood. Tell others of Me in this light. Share with them what they can have in Me – love and freedom without condemnation. Let them know the joy available to them even as imperfect beings.

They must first have an understanding of the basis of our relationship before they can even begin to partake of My gifts and Promises. Do not cripple them by allowing them to think you have always been at your current level of maturity or you have always known Me as you do today. Let them know, under

My direction, how to begin with Me. Then I will do the rest – helping them to grow at their own pace to ultimately come to know Me on a broader scale.

July 24

Oftentimes, I grow weary of the pomposity of the Church/ My Body acting as though it has all the answers, as though it is so mature. This act of superiority only pushes away the rest of the flock. Why would anyone come to Me if they feel their inadequacies will only be pointed out more or heightened? On your own, not one of you is adequate. But with Me, you sit in heavenly places. Examine yourself and realize your role is to edify others and not to exalt yourself as did the Pharisees of old. Be mindful of the work that is at hand.

July 25

Challenges.

Challenges are at hand in the lives of My children. But the rewards are greater than those offered by the world.

Life with Me is a constant process that can be compared to the properties of water. Water has no shape of its own. It merely accepts the shape of the container in which it sits. It evaporates, it can be added to and there is often no distinguishable difference to the naked eye.

In your life with Me, although you remain basically the same outwardly, you are changing on the inside. As you meet each circumstance with My Love and peace, you are becoming more like Me. The world may not recognize the minute changes, but I see them. Then as you continue to exemplify Me, you/your "water" becomes a little more like Me/your "container." As this occurs, the world will then see the change in you as well. Strive to be as liquid filling the curves and crevices of a vessel... and let that vessel be Me.

July 26

The triumph of My children comes first with salvation, then with walking in the love and power I have ordained for them. You have been assigned to triumph, to be victorious over the adversary, over circumstances and over life. For even in physical death you are the conqueror because you then have eternal life with Me.

Think of the major challenges of your life and know you have been selected as the winner. There is no defeat for those in My Family. Tell others so they might understand. I did not plan for them to fight their battles alone nor that they should lose. Tell them that before time, their victories were carefully designed and planned and there is no defeat in Me.

July 27

> **29 Take my yoke upon you, and learn of me; for I am meek and lowly in heart: and ye shall find rest unto your souls. 30 For my yoke is easy, and my burden is light. (Matthew 11:29-30 – KJV).**

Cast your cares upon Me. There is no reason for you to carry the cares of the world on your shoulders. I have said I bear it all and I have told you not to fret or worry, for I am peace. Place all your concerns and worries on Me, for you are not to attempt to handle them on your own nor are you designed to handle them.

Those outside of Me feel that by handling the circumstances which they encounter, they are being responsible citizens. But in My Kingdom, it is different. Yes, you use common sense, for I have given you a brain for this purpose. However, everything is to be turned over to Me first and not at the end when you see things are out of control. Place all in My Hands finding certain peace, and then *I* will move you. This is being a responsible citizen in My World.

July 28

Seldom has the world seen such miracles as they will see in these last days… and all parts of My Body will be used to accomplish these works. Each of you has a role to play and each of you will need to function according to My plan. It is an exciting time and should be shared by all. It will not be, however, because so many are blinded, so many are deaf.

Be ready to move with Me to draw in others, for time is fast running out. Oh, it is an exciting time for My children! Let this excitement extend to all you encounter as you share My Good News!

July 29

I desire a people who will follow Me as their champion, without question, without doubt. So often, you understand rationally that I have fought all battles and won, but in your hearts your understanding is limited. You call on Me believing I can handle some things, however without thought, you leave Me out of other situations.

Know that I can bring you through any circumstance victoriously, and have. Realize as automatically as you take each breath, also is My Breath/My Presence. Understand you need do nothing without Me, for I am always with you leading and lighting your path.

July 30

Looking back over your life and knowing everything "bad" you have done, you may wonder how your parents could still love you. But they not only had an inherent love for you because you were a part of them, they also knew many of your actions were based in growing pains, in phases. They knew one day you would grow into a responsible, mature adult who would then raise your family in much the same way you were raised.

Look at Me as your almighty parent of love. Know that I look at you in much the same way as your earthly parents as you grow into spiritual adulthood. They loved you through all even when you were unaware, and I too, love you through all – on the grandest scale of all.

July 31

And let us not be weary in well doing: for in due season we shall reap, if we faint not (Galatians 6:9 – KJV).

I love you and expect in your attempt to serve Me, you place one foot before the other and not fall away. I expect you to never give up in the face of adversity. I expect you to do the very best you can in your journey with Me. And what can you expect from Me? My complete and utter devotion to you no matter what your outcome.

There is no other love like Mine. Think of your relationships and how your feelings vary depending on what the other person does to you. You might get mad and say hateful things as a result, or withhold your love as punishment. Know that I am not that way, for My deep Love for you never changes because I never change.

AUGUST

August 1

> **[4] "And when he brings out his own sheep, he goes before them; and the sheep follow him, for they know his voice. [5] Yet they will by no means follow a stranger, but will flee from him, for they do not know the voice of strangers" (John 10:4-5 – NKJV).**

When you love Me and are seeking to do My will, you will undoubtedly grow in maturity. And as you mature, you will realize I am becoming more a part of you as you become more like Me. Therefore, if you pray/ask for an answer and a response flashes through you, do not then question was that you, was that Satan, was that God? I know what you think and I know what reinforcements you need in any given situation. I also know how to override any influences of My adversary. So, when you are seeking Me, believe you have received your answer from Me, without contradiction to My Word, until or unless I show you otherwise. I am able to make all clear to you and do, when your focus is on Me. Then, it is up to Me to see that the answer manifests.

August 2

> **Peace I leave with you, my peace I give unto you: not as the world giveth, give I unto you. Let not your heart be troubled, neither let it be afraid (John 14:27 – KJV).**

Release in Me is the purest, sweetest peace you can have. There is no reason for you to suffer in turmoil, confusion or doubt. I have told you that I handle all. I take all your burdens, all your cares. Who else do you know who would do so much for you every moment of every day? Who else do you know who hungers to serve you? Who else do you know who awaits your cry ready to wipe away each tear? Who else do you know?

I love you so very much and have made all provision for your needs to be met, for your burdens to be lifted. Know that your sorrow is My sorrow and I long to bring you to a sharing of joy together. Release all your burdens to Me and begin to move with My *wings of peace*.

August 3

The feast of the Royal Family is fast approaching and oh, what a wonderful time we shall have together! As an heir of the Kingdom, your royal seat has been reserved.

While you await that happy day, you are to live your present life as a member of My Royal Family. You are to live in My Love, peace, righteousness and victory. You are not to exist as a second-rate citizen who is a victim of circumstances. No, you are to live as one who has the Ear of My Father, expecting the blessings of Him now. Reflect on who you are in the Family of God and begin to manifest your position.

August 4

Belief first, then confession.

Your belief in My answer, whatever your request, must be rooted deeply in your heart. Then, your confession through words, thoughts and actions follows. As I have said, all you need do is ask believing, and it shall be done according to My plan. But, many never see their manifestations because a true belief had not yet been formed within them. If you confess something and have to work your belief up, do not expect the instant manifestations you would receive if your firm belief was already there.

At times, you may request something in your mind, and the next moment it is done without your even uttering a sound. That is when you are convinced and your thoughts and/or actions are standing in support of your belief. Move to believe deeply and watch My power to answer your heart's desires move miraculously.

August 5

And other sheep I have, which are not of this fold: them also I must bring, and they shall hear my voice; and there shall be one fold, and one shepherd (John 10:16 – KJV).

Who shall know My Voice? Those who seek Me. There is no lack of clarity and there is no confusion in Me. Seek and you shall find... of that be assured. My Voice extends to all and I desire not to lose one of you.

I am not interested in placing pitfalls in your path. I am interested in drawing all to Me for their ultimate good. It would be the same thing as My telling you that you must walk to the store for your food and giving you no legs to walk there. I would not do that. It is not My intention to make it harder for you to be close to Me – to come to know Me and My power. No. I, as love, desire to use all of My power on your behalf for you to reach full stature in My Family. Therefore, leave all, *all* to Me and know I handle all if you but let Me.

August 6

I take care of all. Never doubt that. Know that whatever you do, believing you are in line with My guidance, will be handled by Me. But, even when you somehow miss it totally, be assured I am there working all to your final good. Because you err, it does not change your heart-form. No. I see your heart and the depth of your love and commitment to Me. And, when you are serious about Me and not simply giving lip service, the heart I see does not change because you made a mistake. I understand this. Now, *you* think on it and understand.

August 7

Make a joyful noise unto God, all ye lands (Psalm 66:1 – KJV).

Merriment and joy are what await you at My Feast. But, until that time, strive always to find joy in each circumstance. Look for reasons to rejoice at all points. As you stretch toward consistent rejoicing, I will become more and more a part of you until it is totally natural for you to see everything with *joy-eyes*. Then, as I have promised, you will truly walk in My strength which grows from My joy.

Squint to see even the slightest reason for joy and soon your eyes will be wide with anticipation of more blessings to come in every situation.

August 8

Glory! Glory! Let the trumpets sound! Begin to think of celebration as you think of Me, for what you have in Me is reason to celebrate. Eternal life, limitless love, power over all... if these are not reasons enough to celebrate, then nothing is. Meditate on your position with Me and let your life-sound be *celebration!*

Too often, you allow your circumstances, people and even emotions determine your ability to celebrate and you lose sight of Me/My blessings. Commit yourself to look neither to the left or right as you walk with Me. Press to your higher calling and celebrate with Me/Us.

August 9

Never ever think you are alone, for I have said I will never leave you nor forsake you. Your full understanding of that is what makes My power in your life work. Realizing that at no time are you out of My care/My protective touch, is of the utmost importance. Then, knowing we share your space jointly, opens the door to your understanding My Presence/My involvement. I, as your God, am entwined with you as I am Father, Son and Holy Spirit together. Meditate on our involvement and begin to comprehend the power at your fingertips. We await your response with great anticipation.

August 10

Whenever you hear My still small Voice, begin to move immediately, for as you respond more and more automatically to My guiding/nudging, the easier becomes our action as one. Often your response is sought only as a lesson in obedience. Other times, it is for a much greater purpose you may never know. But, it is all necessary for our walk together. If you have not shown your response/obedience in lesser situations, how can it be clear with greater ones?

As I know all and know what you will choose, there are still lessons which must be learned for your sake in our walk of oneness.

August 11

Nothing is impossible through Christ Jesus. Anything you ask believing in My Name, it shall be done. There are no limits, no restrictions, no obstacles too great for Me. My Name is above all and it is yours for the asking. I long for your requests, for I have bestowed all to you and so little has been taken. Understand from this moment on that I have done all for you and withhold nothing from you.

Face not your situations alone. When you said "Yes" to Me, we became one, which means you are never alone. Even in your darkest hour, know I am with you working all to your good. Call on Me, your Lifeline for all.

August 12

Spiritual Metamorphosis.

Think of the metamorphosis of a caterpillar to a butterfly – crawling bound to the earth, then transformed in a cocoon to a beautiful winged creature – and know how much more magnificently I transform you. You are bound to earth no longer. Become My spiritual butterfly full of beauty and grace and take wing with Me.

It is time for you to see yourself as I see you and what you will become. You must know by now there are no limits to what I see – past, present or future. So, believe Me when I say you are that beautiful butterfly no matter what you have had to endure, no matter what you have believed. I see the final you and you are magnificent! Believe it, not so you become prideful, but so you understand the stature that is yours. Then, help others to see their transformation, their *metamorphosis*.

August 13

Sweet Love.

As honey which is sweet to the taste, but provides so much more through its natural nourishment – so too, with My Love. It is sweet and tender, but it does not smother. It nourishes you as you grow. I will do anything for you, but I allow you to choose to make your own mistakes. Even knowing the pitfalls, I will not force you to make the right decisions.

My Love is the purest and fullest of all because I desire that you come to your highest level in Me at your own pace. My Love is a love that is always there and knows exactly when to embrace you or when to step aside. It is not easy to love like this, but as the purest love, there can be no other way. Understand My sweet Love for you and know it is always there.

August 14

Mysteries will unfold as we walk together. So many things that seemed foreign to you – foreign in the sense that you never gave a single thought to them or simply could never understand their working – will become familiar friends as we become one.

As we stroll this life together, a whole new world will unfold – the magic of My Creation, the power at hand, the importance of the spiritual realm, the depth of My Love.... Are you not glad to know what was important before you knew Me no longer weighs the same? Are you not glad to know I have taken care of all? Are you not glad to know what you once thought were mysteries no longer are such because you hold the key? Are you not glad...? Rejoice!

August 15

Then shall the eyes of the blind be opened.

It is a time of spiritual awakening, a time of viewing things in a much different light. What you thought you knew and believed wholeheartedly is being revealed in greater depth, with greater clarity.

Opening the eyes of the blind does not only pertain to the unsaved as many have thought. It also applies to the saved who have been living with a kind of blindness... with shadows of Me. Now their eyes are being opened as well. Praise God! And, they are beginning to understand there is much more to My Promises than they were ever aware. They are beginning to see that My Holy Spirit is there to lead and guide them in everything. They are beginning to experience the love of which I have spoken these many years. They are beginning to know My joy is indeed their strength. The scales on their eyes are being removed. And, it is the responsibility of each one of you to help with the operation, to be used as My instrument at My direction to help each to see Me as I have meant it to be.

August 16

"The thief does not come except to steal, and to kill, and to destroy..." (John 10:10 – NKJV).

Guard your heart against the thief, for he wants only to steal, kill and destroy. Never allow it. Never permit it. I am your strength through all, so do not let him deceive you. Never let him blemish our relationship. Understand that I am purity... and as I am in you, so too, are you.

When you begin to hear/think things that you know run contrary to My Word and therefore, contrary to Me, stop them in their tracks and recognize them for what they are – complete deception. Then, take the authority that I have given you and cast them down. Remember who you are. You are not subject to them or the enemy, so do not give place to them.

August 17

Use My Eyes to see beyond the natural things you can see, feel, taste and touch. They are only a small part of what is real. For so long, man has often overlooked what he cannot explain with his physical senses, what He cannot see. But, it does not make what is beyond his grasp unreal.

In your growth with Me, strive to see My World particularly in the face of adversity, for that is indeed where the real world is. As you reach this point, you will see the things of your world change in the twinkling of an eye. Look beyond and see the Truth that surrounds you. My Kingdom is in you and around you.

August 18

The guiding and leading of My Spirit is often so subtle, so simple that most miss it. What I desire is that nothing you do be done without My direction, not only in your specific prayers and requests, but in your day-to-day activities. Your union with Me should be so close and consistent that My Spirit should be turning, pushing or pulling you at any given time. There must be more understanding of this as there should not be the separation/segregation that exists in the lives of most. Tell them.

All in one – you and I. I in you, you in Me. We are one. Oneness – never separated, never apart. Dwell in our life together and know I am ever-present, ever there. All in one, sharing our life as *one*.

August 19

There must never come a time when you are too busy to spend time with Me. As your Master Planner, if we do not talk regularly, how will you know what you are to do? Busy-ness causes separation from Me and My direction. No matter how subtle your busy-ness, always confer with Me first. I do not give you things to do for the sake of doing them. And, I will not give you goals to reach that do not have a higher purpose. Set your priorities with Me first. Then, we will work together more efficiently and effectively than you could ever do or imagine on your own. Set your priority on Me and let all else follow.

August 20

Seldom do you see things exactly as I because you have not the total picture. But, as you strive to become more like Me, as I become more of you, your understanding will grow. Do not ever be discouraged when all seems to go contrary to what you believe, for I am there working all to your good. Think of Me as you would a director of a play, behind the scenes coordinating the actions of all the players. I do much the same, not being seen by the outside world or often even the players, but very much in charge of the overall performance.

Know that all is being handled for your good and I am making all clear to you step by step. Allow Me to direct what will be your greatest performance of all – your life with Me.

August 21

Mineral deposits such as gold or silver are thought of as so invaluable. People build mines as a means of extracting precious substances from the earth. Men even kill each other to possess this priceless treasure. Others risk their lives on a daily basis to go down deep tunnels to mine these deposits. The air is thin, the quarters dark and dirty, often dangerous.

I am the One who created all the silver and gold. I am Light… I am purity and My supply is endless. My gifts to you are more precious than any metal on earth. Why would anyone choose the former without the latter – the object rather than the Maker? How could anyone forget Me in the whole scheme of things?

August 22

Centuries have gone by since My coming and instead of people drawing closer, many have pulled farther away. The time has come for the Church to come together and move as one – to take My Word to the lost, to move and grow in Me.

Through the various tactics of My adversary, the Church has grown to be more and more crippled. I tell you this day, I know who I have chosen and what I have purposed for each life. I stand in authority over it all and press you now to fulfill My plan. Take My authority as your own and let nothing deter you as you take your place with Me. We are almost at the finale and there is much work to do. Be My strong one… give love. Take authority in My Name and intercede. Go forth in My perfect will as it has been ordained for you. Go forth with Me.

August 23

Whether you sin or not does not determine your salvation once you are in My Family. Yes, sin means separation from Me, but remember that as My child, you are also covered by the Blood. When you did something bad as a child in your earthly family, did you fear that you would be thrown out of the family, out of the home? Of course not! You knew you would most likely be punished, but you also knew you would receive forgiveness at some point for your wrongdoing.

Well, do not expect less from Me as your heavenly Father. I said I would lose not one of My chosen, so how could I snatch your salvation away every time you err? I said confess your sins and you shall be forgiven – immediately, without delay. Do not be deceived. I have not intended to lose one of you.

August 24

Learn with Me. Walk with Me. Never go before Me. Never stay behind. Today, many believe they must make their own way. And, certainly faith without works is dead. But, the truth is, often any faith in Me is missing because they are working their own plans without any thought of Me. I cannot be left out of the equation nor do I expect you to lag behind doing nothing.

There must be a constant flowing, a constant touching, so that you can move as I move. Stay with Me as you seek Me. We are one – gloriously moving and growing together.

August 25

> **"You shall have no other gods before Me" (Exodus 20:3 – AMP).**

I am the Lord your God. Let no other gods come before you. So many have no conception of what "gods" means and the various degrees to which things may be their gods. A "god" is anything in which you place your trust or focus – your job, your car, a man, a woman, gambling.... The list is endless. You need not physically bow down before a statue for it to be termed a "god." It is the importance it carries for you spiritually, emotionally and/or physically. Search your heart for your particular gods and seek to remove them, for with their presence is less room for Me.

August 26

Necessary changes.

As you reach to meet each challenge with peace in your heart, know that growth will result. Give reflection to the lessons of your past which caused you to mature. They were usually not easy and most often placed you in an area of discomfort – you would not have selected the situation if given a choice, in retrospect. But, it is the way you learn best, being stretched to overcome situations as you grow into becoming a responsible adult/a credit to society.

So too, it is with Me. You mature spiritually as you overcome obstacles and situations. And in overcoming, lessons can be learned – growth can occur. It may not be instantaneous, as you may have to re-learn and re-learn. But once learned, it will never be forgotten and you will have climbed to another level of maturity in Me. Welcome the challenges for your ultimate growth.

August 27

Marriage in My Eyes is for life. But, the marriage of which I speak is of a spiritual nature – one matched in Heaven. There are relationships that the world labels as marriage, but the one I have ordained and hold most dear is between a man and a woman joined in holy matrimony and bound by their Covenant with Me. This marriage exemplifies My relationship with you as My Bride – one planned before you were in your mother's womb, based in love and commitment with Me at the center. It does not vary based on whether you are good or bad, right or wrong. It is a relationship founded on unwavering love that knows no bounds.

There are many marriages that have not been ordained by Me and lack a solid love foundation. In these cases, their free will has brought them together rather than Me. Even so, My blessings fall upon them as well.

August 28

> **19 "Again I say to you, that if two believers on earth agree [that is, are of one mind, in harmony] about anything that they ask [within the will of God], it will be done for them by My Father in heaven. 20 For where two or three are gathered in My name [meeting together as My followers], I am there among them" (Matthew 18:19-20 – AMP).**

Strength in unity.

Imagine My Church marching as one in My Name against the powers of evil. Remember when I said where two are gathered in My Name I am in their midst? Well, think of the Church finally together and the implication of those numbers. It is a time of breaking down barriers and coming together in Truth.

As you carry My Word forth, strive to unite with others on the Truth, My Truth. Overlook the things that can be overlooked and be as one in the areas which you can. In time, I will clear out the misconceptions to allow the fullest fellowship of My Church. But, for now, do all you can to put aside your prejudices and judgmental attitudes and begin to walk as one.

August 29

Nursing My babies into "tottledom" is what My Body must do. The Church must realize that most are babies in Me and as such, they must be placed on the proper diet for growth. When you look at feeding your own children, you start first with some type of milk, then on to diluted cereals and strained food. Later, as they begin to get their teeth, their diet consists of foods that require chewing until finally, they are eating adult foods.

With the teaching of My Word, there is no difference. My babies must start with the milk or formula, if you will. Then, step by step, they must be brought into the meat of the Word where they ultimately become mature eating adult foods.

It is the responsibility of the Church to help My babies become mature, to assist in their growth by giving My Word

– the Word of God – through a planned program directed by the Holy Spirit. It is not the Church's role to leave babies as babies or be disgusted if growth does not progress at an expected rate. Do all babies (natural) grow at exactly the same speed? No! You are to help My babies *grow* through the teaching of My Word, by word and deed.

August 30

Then shall the eyes of the blind be opened...

It is a time of awakening when many are rising from the deep slumber of darkness into the rays of sunshine. As you move from darkness into the light, you are not able to behold the brightness all at one time and must shield your eyes. So it is when you move from the shadows to the dawn spiritually. You are unable to view it all at once and have to adjust to it gradually. Remember this in your own growth as well as in your work with others.

There are so many misconceptions even with water baptism. It is symbolic of being bathed, immersed in Me. Man has taken so many basic truths and turned the symbol into the reality. Do not be persuaded by these people. They are doing nothing more than misleading and crippling My flock. The rituals, the offices, the work – they mean nothing without My salvation. Tell them. Tell them all!

August 31

Charity begins at home. Do all you can to show My Love to those nearest to you, your family. What better testimony of My Good News than the love displayed at home when you are tired and all facades have been stripped. People so often share love and kindness outside of the home and forget it when they are behind closed doors. No. Share My Love first with your loved ones and then go out. Get your house in order and handle the smaller situations, so I can use you in the larger ones. See what changes need to be made at home and do them in love. Charity, indeed, begins at home.

SEPTEMBER

September 1

There is so much to learn and so little time to accomplish it. Stay with Me as these lessons come. Know I am in control and that we will be moving quickly, like the abbreviated lessons of summer school as opposed to the regular school session. What has taken many a lifetime to learn will now be learned in much shorter periods of time – weeks, months. It is a time of great revelation. Have you noticed? It is time. Do not discount it because it is unfamiliar to you, just receive and allow Me to sort it out for you. Continue to yield and you will learn with Me.

September 2

Who am I? The Son of the Living Father Who is the Creator of Heaven and earth and beyond. And, I sit at His Right Hand petitioning Him for you.

Who/what else do you need? In Me you always have freedom – freedom not to be subject to circumstances, freedom to make the choice to leave all to Me. Do not ever let anyone tell you it is not so. For too long, My people have lived in bondage that they have believed true in their minds – a bondage that has robbed them of their rightful heritage. Do not ever let anyone deceive you into believing that My freedom is not freedom of the purest form. Thank God, you are free at last! Know what it means to be free in Me… and give thanks.

September 3

> **Come unto me, all ye that labour and are heavy laden, and I will give you rest (Matthew 11:28 – KJV).**

Misery and sadness need not be in My Kingdom on earth. My children need never suffer dismay once they learn what it means to fully turn all over to Me. There are not certain situations that you release only to retain others. No. In turning all over to Me, it means giving everything – every problem, every care – to Me.

Once you have grasped the fullness of My Promises – that I take care of everything, that I will never leave you nor forsake you, that I work all together for your good – then you will know the true peace which I have for you. You will know you need not be affected by the ups and downs of daily life. You will finally understand what I request when I ask you to release all to Me.

September 4

But thou, O Lord, art a shield for me; my glory, and the lifter up of mine head (Psalm 3:3 – KJV).

I am your glory and the lifter of your head. When you feel you have been beaten down and cannot go on, rejoice and praise Me because I am lifting you up! Through praise, you are able to experience joy, a joy that knows My power to remove all burdens.

Remember to keep your head high so you may see Heaven and shake off your cares. You should not have your chin on your chest saying, "Woe is me." You should have the peace and joy that comes only through Me. Picture My Hand on your chin lifting your face, your entire being to Me. Look not at your circumstances. Look at Me, because I am indeed the lifter of your head!

September 5

Challenges.

I challenge you to grow, to not give up when you face adversity. I challenge you to walk in faith believing My will, My perfect will is being done. I must have a people who do not faint at each supposed obstacle, for My rewards are great.

Where you have "failed" before in like circumstances, strive to overcome with the strength and authority of true royalty. Welcome each challenge with joy knowing that you are growing stronger in Me and allow Me to release My power to serve you as you face the trials of day-to-day life.

September 6

Shelter yourself in Me against any storm which faces you. I have all that you need and I *am* all that you need. I am whatever you need to overcome. I can be a lean-to in a warm summer storm. I can be a home built to withstand the harshest elements. I can be your fortress in the midst of the storms of war. I can be all. I am all. I AM.

The daily challenges are the ones which most easily cause you to lose your joy. Recognize them and overcome them to regain your joy. Suppose Joseph and Mary had given up in their search to find shelter. But, they did not. They felt that even a stable could prove to be suitable for the Virgin Birth. And *lo… a Savior was born in a manger…* born in the lowliest of surroundings to rise as King of kings and sit with His heavenly Father. They felt the place mattered not, but that they had shelter for their First Born. And I tell you – let no challenge, no disappointment cause you to give up and lose your joy. Find the best in whatever your circumstances and praise your God.

September 7

> **Taste and see that the Lord is good; blessed is the one who takes refuge in him (Psalm 34:8 – NIV).**

Taste and see how good I am. So many look at Me and only see the surface. However, I desire that you delve into Me, that you dig deeper and come to know Me. There is so much more to our relationship than just viewing each other from afar. We are designed to touch, to embrace one another in utmost intimacy until we merge into one. You are no longer you in the old sense – lost and dying before you accepted Me as your Lord. In our life together, you will become more and more like Me until you are one with Me and I am totally in you. Taste and see how good I am.

September 8

Lazarus was raised from the dead after he was laid in the tomb. I have said, "Greater works can be done in the power of My Name." I did not qualify it or limit it for certain situations. I said greater works. So, do not limit Me and My miracle-working power to what you think possible. It is time for a total outpouring of the Spirit to manifest in many ways – in His fullness. Partake.

Why people find it so difficult to release all and realize My death is for today, is hard to understand at times. But My adversary has distorted so much that people cannot believe I have made it so easy. Tell them I am real. Tell them I am the same yesterday, today and forever. Tell them.

September 9

Oneness. Wholeness. Fullness.

My interaction with you is based on our oneness. The more we are one, the more I am able to bless you and the more you are able to receive those blessings. As we grow into oneness, a singleness, you begin to think like Me and act like Me. Your understanding of Me and your position in Me will become clearer and encompass more. You will know why you are to do certain things in certain situations because you will know it is what I would do. And, you will know I am doing these things through you.

As you grow into My wholeness, you take on My attributes as I take on yours... yours in the sense of accomplishing My works through your individual personality, sense of humor and stature. Coming into oneness with Me is what I desire for you/ for us. And once it is achieved, watch My blessings flow!

September 10

Never ever feel I am away from you and do not know exactly what you are facing. I have known since the beginning of time what would be in your life, what you would face. If you believe I am your all-knowing, all-powerful, all-loving Father, why fret at each turn? If you believe I work all together for good, why look on your circumstances with dismay?

My Son and I have been One since the beginning and you and I are one through Him, which will endure throughout Eternity. Your life is Mine and has been planned with the utmost love and attention. Rest in that knowledge of our oneness and rejoice in our love-life together.

September 11

> **Therefore, since the promise of entering his rest still stands, let us be careful that none of you be found to have fallen short of it (Hebrews 4:1 – NIV).**

There is not a moment that goes by that I am not planning/have not planned for you. One of the greatest joys of being with Me is when you finally learn to rest in Me and know deep in your heart I have not overlooked one precious detail of your life. That is when you know the perfect working of your life is more important to Me than even to you. What joy your realization will bring to you and to Me!

Let Me handle those things that I know how to handle – *everything*. I am perfectly designed for this task. Trust Me and in your trusting, praise Me!

September 12

Glory and honor are due Me because I am One with the Father. Never forget that, as we grow together. Remember that while we are one, as your elder Brother, I have a unique position with our Father that you do not have. I have dwelled with Him since the beginning and share His Presence in ways you cannot yet imagine or understand. As you mature in Me, you will realize I am not to be taken for granted/to be used. But at the same time, you will know I am here to serve you at every point. Come to know Me and the beautiful intricacy of our union. Your reverence and desire to serve releases *My* service to you.

September 13

The Father and the Son.

Nickel and dime attitudes have no place in My House of Jewels and the issues at hand need to be addressed with great conviction. Wishy-washy children are not what I desire, so make sure that in our walk together, your belief in what concerns Me is strong and rooted. Then, you will be able to share in the full blessings of My Kingdom.

My Glory exceeds all… the sun, the moon, the stars. As the Creator, I am more than the created. I am *more* than what I have created. And, when we finally reign together in Glory, you too, will be above My creations. Think of all I have in store for you. Think of your place in Me and rejoice!

September 14

Glory and honor are due Me. As you come to know Me and realize I am in *all* things, you will not feel adequate to give Me all of the glory and honor I deserve. You will feel too insignificant to even utter My praises. But praise be unto God – as you grow to know Me, you will know our relationship is not like that. You will know you have access to Me at any time. You will know in Me you are deserving because I love you. You will know you can do all things through Me. And, you will know that your praise is exactly what I desire and is what blesses and moves Me.

Focus on the blessings I have bestowed upon you and let our relationship flow. Know that through Me you are worthy of all.

September 15

It is your responsibility to tend to My flock as My child, but only as My Holy Spirit guides you. It is of the utmost importance that you not take it upon yourself to move without Me. When you do, your words will most likely fall on unreceptive ears or at least less receptive than I had intended. Move only with Me.

Plan to listen to Me more each day and tune your ears to My Voice. It takes practice, so do not be discouraged at your beginnings. But, it is worth the effort because the joy that comes from knowing My Voice is most glorious. Come, let us move as one as we draw in My flock.

September 16

Everything I do is perfect – not too much... not too little... not too soon... not too late – *perfect*. Think about My perfection and understand what it means to be guided by perfection. Think about what it means to have Me, My power, My all, to lead and guide you. As you reflect, understand the complete folly in not yielding to My direction.

When you can have complete perfection in Me, why would you strive to have anything else? Do not accept less than what

I have ordained for you. Know that in Me, you are entitled to the best.

September 17

Through faith in Me, mysteries unfold.

As your faith in Me grows and you come to see My Face, so many things you once questioned will now have answers. Our union makes clear so much that could never be understood before. As you tap into the wisdom and knowledge of the universe through Me, prepare to learn much. Accept it without question, knowing I am filling you and bringing you to a higher plane in Me.

At this juncture, it is so important that you be a faith-walker and not allow the things of this world to determine what is truth for you. Everything about Me is beyond natural wisdom and understanding, but with Me, the veil is lifted and a new reality will become evident to you.

September 18

> **...choose you this day whom ye will serve;... but as for me and my house, we will serve the Lord (Joshua 24:15 – KJV).**

Choose this day who you will serve. It may often feel that you have no choice, but this is not a walk you can base on feelings. The choice has always been and always will be yours. There is no longer time for middle-of-the-road Christians who sit on the fence. Either you are Mine or you are not, for you can never please Me halting between two minds.

You have chosen Me because you have some knowledge of what I offer you, and others must have an opportunity to make their decision as well. Tell them, even show them by your example, all they have in Me and serve as My conduit of love.

September 19

Why do you try to decide what you will and will not believe in the natural realm, when you are unable to clearly see the things of the spirit realm? Have you spent time in sweet communion with Me to even be sure of My Voice? What you see manifesting in the natural is often the exact opposite of what is to come/what I have ordained spiritually. But, as you spend that precious time with Me, I will make it clear to you by My Holy Spirit, for I am not unclear. So, do not rely on what you see. Rely on Me and rely on what you know is Truth, My Truth.

September 20

> **[15] But speaking the truth in love, may grow up into him in all things, which is the head, even Christ: [16] From whom the whole body fitly joined together and compacted by that which every joint supplieth, according to the effectual working in the measure of every part, maketh increase of the body unto the edifying of itself in love (Ephesians 4:15-16 – KJV).**

My Body/the Church is incomplete. In some areas I have "arms" working. In other areas I have "hands" and "feet" working. But until all parts come together as one, My Body will be incomplete. I, as the Head, need all parts to function efficiently because each part, whether a toenail or an eye, plays as important a role as another in My total plan.

My charge to you is to unite with other parts of My Body, coming together on one foundation, Me, and leaving the differences to Me. My Body must be as one and function as a unit with love as its base. Strive to unite one with another as you await My return.

September 21

Love.

The sweetness of My Love is the permeating aroma of My Kingdom. My Love brings life and light to dark, shadowy places – it never changes and never fails. It magnifies the joy-sounds of the universe.

Love is what I seek from you – love for Me first, then for others. Love… love that causes you to submit yourself to Me without question, love that loves the unlovely without thought of what you receive in return or what someone else may think. Your love throws wide the doors of My patient, waiting Love for you. Give it now to receive it. *Love.*

September 22

Lessons… lessons… lessons.

It is a time of lessons for My children. My lessons will come fast and challenge you to a higher understanding of Me. I tell you this so you will not be confused when a generally accepted interpretation or definition is no longer satisfactory. I want you to gain a fuller appreciation of My Word, My Promises. In order for growth to occur, you will find yourself being challenged by situations and circumstances. But, hold on and be strong! It is all part of the process and your resulting strength and revelations will serve to bring you closer to Me, and that is as it should be.

September 23

> **[23]The steps of a *good* man are ordered by the Lord, and He delights in his way. [24]Though he fall, he shall not be utterly cast down; for the Lord upholds *him with* His hand (Psalm 37:23-24 – NKJV).**

Like the steadiness of the feet of a mountain goat, your steps are always sure in your walk with Me – there is never any need for uncertainty or unsteadiness when I guide your steps. It is time for all who love Me to come to understand the simplicity yet intricacy of the relationship I offer. I am here to lead you in all things, not just big or troublesome things. I am totally involved in your life and am directing everything connected with you, even things of which you are basically unaware. My purpose is to be with you always, at all times and in all things. Think on this Truth, learn it and pass it on. I am the same for all.

September 24

Let the joy of your knowledge of Me ring clear in every situation thereby letting others know you have something different. Besides the strength which it provides for meeting each day's challenges, joy draws people like the sunlight draws the beginning of the day's activities. Show what it means to be My new creature. Show the goodness of it – joy unspeakable, full of glory.

Finding joy in daunting situations – senseless killings, ruthless disease, betrayal – can seem beyond anything you can humanly do. But, I tell you this day, you are equipped to have joy in any and all circumstances. How? By choosing to look to Me with the understanding that I know all and can bring you through any trial – *any trial* with joy. The choice is yours.

September 25

There is no need to justify your mistakes when you belong to Me and are in My Kingdom. There will be times when things will not work out as you expect, but you need never be concerned about saving face with Me. Remember, I already knew about it before you did. Just bring all your cares, worries, slips and sins and cast them on Me. I cover it all – Jesus' Blood was shed for that purpose. Realize what we have is love and life together and anything less must be cast out.

As My child, it is imperative that you never focus on the things of the world or what you see around you. You are to walk in the Spirit knowing you are sanctified from the world, knowing that because you see something does not make it so. If you falter, know that I am here to pick you up, dust you off and carry you higher. No matter the situation, each day plan to walk more and more by faith and less by sight. Herein lies the key to your knowledge of Me/My Kingdom.

September 26

In your walk with Me, do not be surprised at the speed with which situations move. One minute your plight may seem impossible and the next minute it has done a complete about-face. That is how it is with Me, working in unseen, amazing ways to bring your utmost good. And, what I want when it occurs is for you to give thanks, to sing My praises and let others know that I do indeed work all things together for good for each of you. I desire that all may come to recognize Me in every single situation, and that nothing is left to chance or luck.

Are you glad we are together? Praise Me!

September 27

All I expect of you is the best you can do at any given time. If you fall short, understand that I knew you would and I am always there to pick up the pieces for a brand new you. Nothing hurts Me more than your pulling away when you err… when you feel I would not understand your behavior and therefore turn from Me. Jesus died and bore all separation, so you would never have to experience it no matter what you have done. Realize I knew all about you – past, present and future – and I still chose you. Choose to remain with Me no matter what, for with Me each day starts anew.

September 28

> **My sheep hear my voice. I know them, and they follow me (John 10:27 – NRSV).**

When I call, listen. Train your ear to hear Me whether it is in the form of a still small Voice or a Voice so loud, you think someone near you is speaking. I have much to say, but I will go unheard if you have not prepared yourself to listen or do not even expect Me to speak to you. So many think that I do not speak today and each day I yearn to be heard. But, you have heard. Now, commit yourself to listen more each day, so we can move, truly move together and show others the Truth.

You know My Love knows no bounds. Therefore, let the light of My Love shine through you.

September 29

As I have mercy for you, be merciful to others. Too often, the hurting who come seeking My Face, are hurt more by those who say they are Mine. The hard heart, the unforgiving heart, has no place in My Church. It cripples, wounds and alienates My Body and it must cease.

Move in My Love as you encounter each person whether in the Body or not. Plan to be loving to one more person each day and soon you will know what it is to walk in love, to be merciful, to be forgiving. Strive to walk as I did, for in giving more, the more you receive.

September 30

The time has come for you to operate in the power I have given you, to utilize it as regularly and comfortably as you eat, drink and sleep. You are not to be bound by this world. Instead, you are to stand victoriously above it, outside of it because My Kingdom is boundless, limitless.

For too long, My children have lived like the world, far beneath their inheritance/their destiny. It is time to free yourself from the bounds of this world and reach the heights I have always intended for you. My power is yours. Realize it and use it, not to pat yourself on the back and bask in your great wonder, but to bless others to My Glory. What I give to you is always to give to others, and in so doing, you receive more than ever imagined.

OCTOBER

October 1

Praise God!

You are My child and I am in control of all things. Just follow Me, love Me and yield to My sweet direction... for all is well. All is well. There is no need to fret or worry. I am in control. As I led My children through the desert, so will I lead you. But, your way will be easier than theirs if you are obedient to Me. There are such great things in store for you – such wonders! Hallelujah!

Take My Hand and grasp it tightly as I lead you down a straight path. Look neither to the right nor the left. Only look to your fellowship with Me – praying, praising and worshipping Me forever. Many people will have to learn they have nothing of any value without Me. Praise Me! Praise Me!

October 2

> **Ye are of God, little children, and have overcome them: because greater is he that is in**

you, than he that is in the world (1 John 4:4 – KJV).

Do not allow Satan to steal your joy. You are My child and all things are working together for good no matter what you see or feel. Praise Me! Take heed of My Word. There is no need to worry because I am taking care of all. Be alert, for you know not where he/Satan will strike. I tell you this so you will not worry, but so you will be prepared in Me.

You know My Voice and how to follow it. Move as *I* say move and be not fearful. You need not be concerned about anyone or anything except Me and My Love and guidance. Take My Hand and let Me lead you – I will not lead you astray. My Heart is the same today, yesterday and tomorrow and has always favored you. By the same love, My guidance is the same today, yesterday and tomorrow and will never vary or be inconsistent with My Word.

October 3

Where I go, you are to follow.

That is how My entire universe is designed. I lead. You follow. I will never leave you or lead you down a crooked path. But, if you have not yielded to Me, you will not be aware of My Presence and take yourself down a path I have not planned for you. I am here as your Head, as the Head of the Body. Your role is to take My lead and follow. Trust Me, for I will never, never lead you astray.

I desire that you walk with Me and you talk with Me. I desire from this time forth your complete attention. Put Me first in good times and times of challenge and all else will be ordered according to My plan. Glory to God!

October 4

Necessary changes.

I never intended for you to stay in the same place and become stagnant. My Kingdom is vibrant, alive! My intention has always been for you to stretch beyond what is known to you even when it may be uncomfortable. Be assured it is not to punish you or make life difficult for you, but necessary for your greater good.

Know that each situation, each challenge you face serves to bring you to a new level of intimacy with Me. Welcome each situation with joy, knowing you are becoming more fully matured. Rejoice in each encounter, knowing it has not occurred by chance. Sing hallelujah, knowing I have planned all for you that we may ultimately become one.

Love is grand, especially when it is *My kind* of love.

October 5

Traveling with Me is not the easiest of tasks, but it is the only way to travel. Yes, there will be trials, temptations, challenges. But in Me, you are victorious. The road has been made clear for you and there are no stops. I am committed to walk with you always.

We have much work to do so as not to lose the unsaved. Your life, your words must be a testimony not only to the unsaved, but to the saved as well. It is time for them to learn how to have Me in every part of their lives instead of a church part or a prayer part. There should be no separation and it is critical for them to see how to have Me in *all* parts. Show them... quietly at times and boldly at others. I will show you how and when.

October 6

My Love is the medicine of the universe for healing all wounds and diseases, so learn to move with My Love in *all* situations. As love becomes more and more your persona, you will see My miracle-working power begin to move and how My Love changes things. You will see how walls crumble when faced with My Love. Seek to become more and more My Love-child as you move throughout the day.

My Spirit is in you – we two, you and I. As I sent My disciples out two by two, so are we. You are never alone, never without My all-powerful Presence. You and I together as one – see the glory in our *glorious union!*

October 7

My children have for so many years been loaded down with the cares and burdens of this world. They have been living in bondage as My children did in Egypt for so many years while subject to the whims of their earthly masters. I say now for you as did Moses before, "Let My people go!" You are not to live in a state where you are controlled by this world. No! I have brought you out of this servitude. I have led you through the desert. I have brought you into the land of milk and honey. Understand and partake.

Do not deny Me by walking in fear and unbelief. Understand your place in Me and what I have done for you, so you may live in your royal inheritance now and forevermore. You are not to serve the world, as your service should only be to Me. When you commit your service to Me, you are then able to stand with My Son at My Right Hand.

Know who you are and stand.

October 8

> **... I am come that they might have life, and that they might have it more abundantly (John 10:10 – KJV).**

I came that you might have life and have it more abundantly. I am life, light and love. I am peace, plenty and power. I am and always will be your all. There is nothing that I will not do for you because I am your source for all.

Nothing will interfere with My Father's plan for you, not even you. Do not try to figure everything out, just walk in faith. There are no problems too large for Me to overcome, so stop questioning everything and follow your inner witness, the Holy Spirit.

You know how your telephone is hooked to a main computer or system. Well, I am that Computer. Sometimes you call Me, other times I call you. Messages are sent regularly, often unbeknownst to you. Therefore, when you know that you know and it is in line with My Word, stand on it. Satan will always try to change you and make situations appear cockeyed, but it is not so. Stand on that witness and do not waver.

October 9

Peace I Am. Peace I bring to you. There is no reason in your walk with Me that you should ever allow yourself to remain in an unsettled state – to be full of fret and worry. I am your peace. I stand with you awaiting your petition for My/Our assistance. Yes, *our* assistance because even the angels await your bidding.

Place all your cares on Me. My Shoulders are not too weak nor My Arms too short that I cannot handle all. Actively seek to remove anything that robs you of your peace and place it on Me. I am above all and therefore, as My Joint Heir, have given you the victory over all that comes against you. Peace I Am.

October 10

Miracles do indeed occur today. They are, in fact, for today. Your belief in Me activates this power. Not your decision that a miracle will happen at a given time, but your faith that I can do it with your knowledge of My will and timing. And, in My perfect way, the miracle will manifest in the best possible way.

Believe in Me and allow Me to work, thereby releasing My miracle-working power.

I will show you great wonders beyond your wildest dreams. Stick close to Me and I will use you in ways yet to unfold. Stay close, for I will use many if they but stay close to Me, yielding... loving... not limiting.

I *will* raise up a people.

October 11

People will come and go, but I am *always* there. Some people are not as far along in their walk with Me as you think. Others are further along than you realize. Look at each walk for yourself through your eyes of love and know them by their fruit. So many of My children need to experience My Love through you and know that it never fails.

Life is short on earth, but with Me, it is eternal. And, My Love can fill all voids – replace the absence of other love. Let Me fill all of your voids/empty places. Although love/life on earth is so temporary, through loving Me, you tap into My Love which is forever. It is difficult for you to understand because it is so all-encompassing, it is almost impossible to conceive. But, do not worry – you are experiencing a part now – all later.

October 12

My desire is that you come to know Me more each day, each hour, each minute. My desire is that in your growing knowledge of Me, you not keep it bound inside of you, but allow it to flow forth to one and all in every situation. This is what arouses the curiosity of the unsaved or even My babes. They begin to wonder what it is that causes My mature ones to rejoice in the face of adverse circumstances or when they have been treated poorly. Man's nature is to want to be happy, but he is seeking it in ways apart from Me. Therefore, seeing your joy in our relationship has great drawing power to those who do not know Me or know Me in the smallest ways.

Come to know Me and share it with others. Be My light to those in the various shades of darkness and help them experience Me to the fullest.

October 13

Then shall the eyes of the blind be opened...

Think of My joy when I see My creations/My children finally able to see Me – watching them grope around in darkness and suddenly able to see My light. I say suddenly, for it will seem that way to them as someone turning on a bright light. But for Me, I have planned it for them since before time began which makes the wait worthwhile. Oh, how I await that day!

I am the Light. Rejoice and bask in it. Stretch toward it as plants reach out to their natural sunlight. They *know* it is life-giving and they need it to survive. So it is with My light for you. I am your survival.

October 14

Think of yourself when you awake in the early morning, eyes still full of sand, attempting to adjust to the early morning light. What I am doing in My Body is much the same… many who have been asleep in Me are now awakening to Me. They, however, are unable to see Me fully for they must adjust to Me in the same way their eyes adjust to natural light. As they awaken, there will be certain lessons they must learn before they can go to the next level of understanding. But, with this step-by-step process, they will finally view Me more fully with eyes wide.

Remember it is a process and each has his plan. Do not become frustrated if someone cannot see Me the same way you can. It is done in My time and in My way. And, remember also you may not see Me as fully as another. Realize I have planned for all and am guiding each one. Walk with Me in that knowledge.

October 15

My children perish for lack of knowledge. It is My charge to you that you teach My children. Share Me with My flock and bring the reality of Me to the world. Let them then decide whether they will be with Me or not. Let it be their choice, not yours.

I want you to be a lighthouse to those on troubled waters, to be a shining star in the night. There is much work to do and so little time. People need to know My Word, My Love. If they know of My Love, then all else will come in My walk with them – in our *holiness* walk, if you will.

I want everyone to know I will work with them and through them, and make miraculous changes overnight. They only need to love Me enough to yield their bodies/souls to Me.

October 16

So whether you eat or drink or whatever you do, do it all for the glory of God (1 Corinthians 10:31 – NIV).

You are to love Me each day, each hour, each minute, each second of your life. You are to be a testimony to Me in everything you do. Remember Me in all things, is what I told My disciples and is what I again say to you. In all that you do, there should I be. There should be no separation from Me in the various parts of your life. Your heart should never leave Me nor the things of Me whether you are at work or play. I am ever-present and as such require your awareness and action.

Ours is a loving relationship which should grow stronger each day. The world neither knows of it nor has anything that compares to it. Try never to push our relationship away. However, if you do, I will be here waiting for your return. *I love you.*

October 17

I will raise up a people who will go forth in My Name looking neither to the left nor the right – My people, ready to do battle with My adversary.

Speak boldly of My Word and I will guide you and show you the Truth. Do not be intimidated because I am love, not fear. Yes, I have made it simple, but there are many who still seem to want it more difficult and have changed My Word to fit their beliefs. It is simple – I love you, you love Me. I will lead you, bless you and purify you. Is that not enough?

Do not ever worry about someone else getting more attention from Me than you because I will give you as much as you will let Me. Open the doors to My blessings and leave them open. I will work more and more with you as you allow Me. Only the narrowness of your vision limits what you receive.

October 18

> **But let him ask in faith, with no doubting, for he who doubts is like a wave of the sea driven and tossed by the wind (James 1:6 – NKJV).**

This is a time of walking in faith and not by sight, a time of not doubting My all-powerful ways. And, in believing that it is I, you know to stand firm. There has been too much wavering, too much inconsistency in the past. I need a Body committed to Me – serving Me by reaching out to the lost.

I am not here to be your buddy just when it is convenient to you. I am to be with you always, in good times and in bad times. It is a time of declaring your faithfulness to Me. Either you are Mine or you are not, as I have little use for the fence-sitter who shifts with whatever is "in" at the time. I am seeking a yielded Body to do My will because it is the only way by which you may truly see Glory-land here on earth.

October 19

Shall we gather at the river?

Water is the life-blood of all My creations. You must have water to survive. Your body is composed predominantly of water. Plants and animals need water for their physical well-being. And, even with the simplest of creatures, they *know* that water is necessary for their survival.

The same is true spiritually of My Water, My Holy Spirit. Water My Word continually, and let the Water of My Word flow through you and give you the life I designed for you. Is it not interesting that in the physical world, lowly animals are equipped to do what is necessary for their survival while man who has been created above all creatures does not use what I have given freely for his spiritual survival? Think on this.

October 20

Take time to smell the roses. Look at the world around you and see it through My Eyes knowing I have accounted for each and every one. What you see around you was not the result of some random bombardment of atoms or a plan of so-called Mother Nature. No, I did it. I planned it from the beginning and continue to do so. Move your eyes off self and realize My ability to create all of the beauty surrounding you.

Know too, I am able to handle all. My desire is that in realizing My Omnipotence and perfection, you will allow Me to use you to bring more beauty to the world as was intended originally.

October 21

It is permissible to be "only human" as the saying goes, just do not wallow in self-pity. Someday you will not have to deal with such things, but for now, you are human and as such have trials and tribulations. My adversary loves to see My children down on themselves when they feel they have not done something quite right. You are My child and as such are under My Grace. I choose not to see your errors when I know your heart is Mine and you are trying. I love you. I am not looking for things to make you feel unworthy. I want you to know the joy of My Grace/Love/Salvation, to know you are not condemned in My sight.

October 22

Never be discouraged when the things around you appear as though they are going contrary to your prayers. Never ever think your prayers are not being answered, for it is at that time, especially at that time, when a total manifestation is about to break forth. Most often, My adversary is making a last-ditch effort to confuse you enough to lose faith so your blessing may be stolen. Think of Daniel and how he had to wait twenty-one days for an answer while the enemy attempted to keep him from receiving it in an unseen heavenly battle. In the end, help came and his prayer was answered. Know that I am in charge and do, indeed, answer your prayers, which are Mine as well.

October 23

If ever you need Me, I am there. I am never more than a breath, a thought, a prayer away. Know that as you are, so am I. I await your need, your desire to spur My action. Know that I will never leave you nor forsake you – not occasionally or seldom – but *never*. Are you hearing Me? I am ever-present, always there because of love.

I love you. Do not ever question My Love, for it is always there… deeper, stronger than you can ever know. My way is love. Do not let anyone tell you otherwise. And through love, your love for Me and Mine for you, I can do all things. Do not limit Me. Allow Me to use My miracle-working power in your life.

October 24

You need never resist Me – only Satan. My Word is Truth, My Word is Love. Realize your Source and you will never have doubts. When it is said, it is done. Only your interference can slow the process. I want you to be happy, to use your life as a testimony to the lost. Do not doubt or fear because it is done.

Make room in your heart for Me. As your heart pumps life through your physical body, your spiritual heart provides life and vitality to you spiritually. Your spiritual heart is where your faith and beliefs lie. It is where you have decided what your commitment to Me will be. It is the place from which My kind of love emanates to others. The fullness of Me in your "heart" determines your entire walk with Me. Open up your "heart" and allow Me to be your true Life-Blood.

October 25

I am your Rock. I am there for your every need and stand the test of time. Most Christians speak of Me as their Rock, but they have no real concept of what it means to have Me as their Rock. I am a Rock on which everything must be placed, a Rock that willingly desires your burdens, your troubles, your cares. I cannot be your Rock, your strong foundation, if you turn to everyone/everything else before you even consider looking to Me. No. If I am truly your Rock, then I implore you to treat Me as such consistently – not just when you feel you have no other options. Think about this word "rock" that is used in reference to Me and begin to understand what it means. I am your Rock – sturdy, strong, unmoving. Place all on Me and stand.

October 26

Innocuous experiences do not make you grow. Only through life-stretching encounters do you grow. Only through your daily encounters do you mature. And, the more I give you, the more I require. You are experiencing a training period – a period of preparation for the work which is required of you. I have not forgotten you nor have I left you, for I have carefully planned all for you. Recognize Me and know you are being honed for My greater purpose. What you are living now is what I require for My perfect plan. Either you are yielded to Me for My direction or you are not. Which will it be?

Come up to Me and meet Me on My level. I am calling you up, not down. It is the only way we can be one, truly one. This is what I mean when I say I will raise up a people... a people who meet Me not on a physical plane, but on a heavenly plane – stretched through circumstance.

October 27

> **For the children of Israel walked forty years in the wilderness, till all the people that were men of war, which came out of Egypt, were consumed, because they obeyed not the voice of the LORD... (Joshua 5:6 – KJV).**

My people were nomads in the desert for forty years because of their disobedience to Me. They wandered for years when it should have been a very short journey. Even so, I cared for them and met their needs although they were not steadfast in Me.

Today, as My spiritual Israel, I do the same for you because I never change. Although you may be disobedient and make things more difficult for yourself, I will never leave you. I will let you make your mistakes, but be assured that I am always there turning all to your good as you allow Me. Your trip may be longer and more difficult than necessary due to your choices, but as I brought My children of Israel into the Promised Land, so I do with you. Know I am with you, blessing you in all circumstances while you strive to walk the straighter path with Me.

October 28

The nearness and reality of Me is a phenomenon most neither recognize nor are aware. Your charge/role in life is to love Me first and share My Love with others – and to do it under, *only* under My direction. All else is secondary. Continue to tell Christians and non-Christians alike of My Love. Sometimes, it is so difficult to tell who is who or what is what. Many Christians have less joy than those who are not saved by My Grace/have not accepted Me. That is not the way a relationship with Me should be. Those in My Family should be joyous, victorious and full of love. But, so often it is just the opposite.

At other times, many who have known and loved Me have been blessed and then have forgotten Me, so there is little difference between them and the world. This must change! I am raising up a people who honor My priorities. The others must change or live with the consequences.

October 29

> **[38] For I am convinced that neither death nor life, neither angels nor demons, neither the present nor the future, nor any powers, [39] neither height nor depth, nor anything else in all creation, will be able to separate us from the love of God that is in Christ Jesus our Lord (Romans 8:38-39 – NIV).**

You are always at home with Me. If you are truly communing with Me, there should never be embarrassment about your shortcomings. I knew of them before you knew even of yourself, and yet I chose you to be with Me. Realize I know all and have always known all. Therefore, anything you do can never come as a surprise to Me. Did I not say I would never leave you nor forsake you? Then, why should you allow embarrassment/disappointment in yourself to separate you from Me?

As you grow to know Me more, it is a process – you understanding more of Me and Me released to do more in you. You will make mistakes, of that there is no question. But, the growth that comes out of your errors is what is important to Me. As you grow more into Me, I am able to use you more for the completion of My perfect plan. I love you. Do not be insecure, for in Me is all security.

October 30

I will give you what you need and more. Do not fret or worry ever. It is important that you stay in My Word. I cannot speak to you as clearly when you do not have My Word as your balance/your weight and measure. Do not allow yourself to be sidetracked. There can be but one focus – Me. I will show you all as I will everyone, if they but listen.

I cherish the love of each one of you. As your love for Me grows, it causes Me to pulsate as a heart pumps blood full of fresh oxygen to the natural body. Your love releases Me to pump more into your life – more blessings, more knowledge, more love, more life. It is the Life-Blood of the Body. Your love as oxygen given to Me, your heart, then My power and Promises as your blood returned to you for abundant life. *Full cycle.*

October 31

> **Not that I speak in respect of want: for I have learned, in whatsoever state I am, therewith to be content (Philippians 4:11 – KJV).**

Contentment is a state of being. It is not something that should vary according to a circumstance. If you are content, it is what you are. As a member of My Family you should be such, for you know I have planned all for you. Strive toward this end.

When your focus is on Me, all things then fall into place. I am here to take all your worries, your cares. If you slip and fall, do you know I still love you? You *know* I still love you, so do not turn your back on Me. I will always be there to pick you up and raise you higher no matter the circumstance. My Love is so extraordinary there are no words to fully explain it. Suffice it to say I will always be there to guide you, to support you, to love you. Stay with Me and learn these truths. Focus on Me and you will see that My Love is easy. Yet, others would have Me as a tyrant demanding this and demanding that when My demands are all based in love… a love relationship that causes you to submit from love rather than fear. Praise Me!

NOVEMBER

November 1

Love, honor and obey Me.

I am the One, the Only. With Me you cannot go wrong. Many talk of fearing Me, but "honor" is a much better word than "fear" because as you love Me, you will want to honor Me/obey Me. Therefore, as you love, honor and obey Me, there is no need to fear Me. And, how do you learn these things? By studying My Word and spending sweet time in fellowship with Me, experiencing My Love and care for you. Once you commit yourself to doing it, you will find it is not hard.

Take time to learn of Me. I am peace. I am love. Taste and see, for I am as honey – sweet, sweet. Oh, so sweet!

November 2

Awaken My children and come into the fullness of My light. Move from hibernation into My full activity. My Body has on the whole been asleep, in an almost comatose state. It is time now for their eyes to be opened to allow Me to stretch them so they can begin to move as full-fledged members of My Kingdom. It is time for each of you to wake up and begin to comprehend My fullness to move as I intended.

I love you and all those around you. It is so good to see many seeking Me/listening for Me. It makes everything worthwhile; all of the rejection, all of the fear... only to be returning into My outstretched Arms for the relationship which has always been theirs.

People are so *funny*. They make everything so difficult, so complicated. Things in life may be difficult from time to time, but what I offer is anything but difficult. I offer love, guidance, protection, victory – everything to make life simple. Yet, many complicate it with Satan's help. Continue to stand in faith and My Promises shall be yours. Claim them all from morning till night with peace, not anxiety and know it is *done*.

November 3

Precious Blood.

My precious Blood covers all. There is no sin too great that cannot be covered/removed by My Blood. When you sin, My Blood not only covers you, but it erases My remembrance of that act or thought. I cast it all into the Sea of Forgetfulness. Never let the enemy deceive you. There is no sin too great for My all-cleansing power. So many have been fooled into believing they could not possibly be forgiven and they stray away from Me. No! Be not deceived! I have made provision for all as I know your nature. There is no sin too great to warrant our separation. *Amen.*

November 4

Spirits connected as one.

Your spirit connected with Mine, yours with others, Mine with all. When you are truly linked by My Spirit to your earthly partners, their moves become yours and yours become theirs. It is strictly involuntary and cannot be forced. As I am in you, so are you in each other. It is the closest bond that exists – unseen but seen... untouchable with the human hand, but stronger than any bond known to man. Know that I have provided this bond for you.

I am not speaking of natural affection, but of a bonding which is first and foremost in the spiritual realm and overflows into the realm/plane with which you are familiar – where your senses tell you what is and what is not.

In the spiritual realm, there is no beginning and no end. It just is. Is it not worth waiting for these relationships to manifest to the world when you know they always have been, will always be and were planned by Me? Is it not worth the patience it takes for this most magnificent union?

November 5

For your Maker is your husband — the LORD Almighty is his name... (Isaiah 54:5 – NIV).

I am your Husband first and foremost. All else must follow. Do not allow yourself to place anything/anyone before Me as it would end in futility and not as I have planned. The temptations to do otherwise are great, but stay the course.

My way is neat and orderly, filled with love. There are never any loose ends when I have handled all. If you do not see the tidiness of this pattern in your life, stop and turn all over to Me. Allow Me to pull your frayed edges together for your good. Let Me be the loom that weaves all the threads of your existence into one magnificent fabric. Let Me be the Designer of your life.

November 6

Take My Hand and I will lead you to Paradise. What does that bring to mind? Beauty. Peace. Serenity. Love. That is what I am... *all* that is good.

Focus on Me as I am not the author of confusion, Satan is. When it is not clear what you are to do, concentrate on Me – stand still, listen and wait. That is all you need do.

I love you so much. My Love is boundless and flows through every part of My Existence. How can anyone run from My Love? They obviously do not know or understand the depth and breadth of My unconditional Love. Tell them as much as you know and understand. Tell them what is in store for them, with Me and without Me. They must know great things are in store for them.

Never question that which you know.

November 7

Prayer is not so much what you say, but your posture, your focus in communicating with Me. You need not say it out loud nor begin a certain way. It is a flowing out to Me of your thoughts, your requests. Then, as you know your prayers are answered in a spiritual flow which comes back to you, you continue giving your thanks to Me. It is a full cycle.

Fasting is also so misunderstood. Again, it is a posture, a wholeness of your being focused on Me your Savior/Intercessor/High Priest. You are in an attitude of communion with Me when your spirit and Mine touch because you have cleaned out the muck and mire. Fasting is not something pertaining just to food. It is a spiritual cleansing in which you lay yourself, your requests and what is in you on the Throne.

You would not go to a king's palace without bathing first, would you? Well, you should not come to My House without bathing yourself internally, spiritually. Fasting from food is not the only way this can be achieved, but it is a way for many of you to better place your focus on Me. Fasting as I intended should be total – spiritual and natural. It should not only be abstinence from food, but abstinence from the things of the world, things of My adversary. And ultimately, you do without so you are able to give to others in the best possible way.

November 8

Often when situations look bleakest, I am doing My mightiest work. It is then you must hold on and walk by faith and not by sight. It is then you must fight the good fight of faith. It is then you must stand on My Promises without wavering – knowing everything is moving according to My plan. Be assured of your victory in Me.

I cannot tell you everything because it is a learning/growing experience for you. I will tell you what you need to know, however, in due time and always right on time. What I require in this process is that you prepare yourself to listen and obey. I will *never* leave you nor forsake you.

November 9

Your will linked to Mine in a position of humility will result in an anointing that causes your thoughts/desires to be manifested. Why? Because you will know My will so well, so clearly, your desires will exactly mesh with My perfect timing, My perfect will. It is toward this end which you should strive – your thoughts as Mine, My thoughts as yours; stretching to My divine purpose – *perfection*.

I hear your thoughts as if spoken aloud. Your speaking things into being is for the ears of the universe – you, those under, those on and those over the earth including My enemy. However, never fear speaking, for death and life manifest in your words. But, at the same time, know also you have a heavenly language by My Spirit which is for My Ears alone. Use what I have given you to loose and bind the things of this world.

November 10

> **[16] And Jesus, when he was baptized, went up straightway out of the water: and, lo, the heavens were opened unto him, and he saw the Spirit of God descending like a dove, and lighting upon him: [17] And lo a voice from heaven, saying, This is my beloved Son, in whom I am well pleased (Matthew 3:16-17 – KJV).**

When we were down at the river being baptized in the water – oh, it was so *beautiful* – the dove descending was symbolic of My Father's Hand on Me. John did not actually see the dove. It was symbolic for want of a better word. Pure, white and light; to show him I was, am and will be – to show My Spirit/My Father's Spirit is in you and *is* recognizable… a dove lighting on you as on Me.

Do not miss the significance of water baptism by focusing on the action. Know that My Father has chosen to place His Hand on you by allowing His Holy Spirit to light on you and dwell in you. You then, by being baptized are proclaiming your newness in Him and your submission to Him. Unfortunately, water baptism has become a ritual in many churches ignoring its true significance. It was never intended to be so.

November 11

"...the people living in darkness have seen a great light; on those living in the land of the shadow of death a light has dawned" (Matthew 4:16 – NIV).

It is important that you not judge or react to what you see on the surface. As My child, use your gifts to discern what is underneath – the state of the heart and whether My Spirit is alive in that person. By doing this, you will promote the unity that I must have in My Church and not split over outward differences. I expect you to grow to rise above these things and see what is true/what is real spiritually. Then receive your blessings.

I desire that you see Me in your sisters and brothers, in the rest of the Body. Even the smallest light should be recognized as Me and related to as such. If you would remove self and let My Spirit interact with the spirit in others, there would be less hurt feelings, fewer problems and continual joy. Stop looking at the outside and begin to see others with your spiritual eyes. See them the way I see you. It is only right that it should be so in My Family.

November 12

Oh, most glorious day!

This is the day that I have truly made. Realize no matter what your earthbound eyes see, it is a day that has been made in Heaven – diligently planned since the very beginning.

Dwell on the fact that what you see is only a minute portion of what actually is. Know that more is going on in areas unseen than in those areas seen by your naked eye. Regardless of how situations appear, rejoice in the knowledge that your heavenly Father is working all to your good, so you can join with Me and say, "Oh, what a glorious day! I shall rejoice and be glad in it!" Hallelujah!

November 13

> **Praise ye the Lord. O give thanks unto the Lord; for he is good: for his mercy endureth for ever (Psalm 106:1 – KJV).**

In your walk with Me, you will find yourself in situations which will make you question how you ever arrived there. But, do not concern yourself with the how's and why's – only be assured that I am in charge and My Mercy endures forever. Know with all clarity that My Grace is sufficient and covers a multitude of sins. Many would have you believe that My Mercy and Grace have no merit and are not enough. But, they are wrong and must be shown/told.

My precious child, be certain of the care I have for you. I sacrificed My only Son for you. As God of all gods, do you think I did not account for all of your actions? Do you think I would leave you with no way out or with no direction? No! Be satisfied in the knowledge that you need only listen for My Voice/My direction and you will know what to do. Focus on what I desire of you and follow My instruction. And, I will handle the how's and why's.

November 14

You need never know where you will take your next step, where I will lead you. Just agree to be My willing vessel and know My Hand is over all. When a sculptor is commissioned to do a bust from a piece of marble, seldom would you be able to tell what the final product will be by looking at it in its early stages. But, when he is finished, what you see is then recognizable, often beautiful.

So it is with Me. I take you in your various sizes and shapes, and carve something brand new and beautiful... unrecognizable in the beginning, but resulting in a replica of Me. You were created in My Image. Never forget that and let My Hand do its work in making you what I have intended, what I have planned.

November 15

> **That was the true Light which gives light to every man coming into the world (John 1:9 – NKJV).**

Now in the beginning, there was Light because I existed. I am Light. *I am, was and will always be Light*. Where I am, there has always been Light and darkness has no place. Your charge this day is to continue My legacy of Light and Love and share them wherever you go, wherever you are – at work, at play or at home – *anywhere*. It is time now to dispel the darkness of the world with the light that you carry. Do not doubt My power in you. The darkness has to flee.

When you make that choice to be with Me and serve Me, then you are welcome to receive all that I Am and all that I have – My Love, My Light, My power, My knowledge, My wisdom. Everything I have is yours. Now, walk in it!

November 16

A sin is a sin is a sin.

So many today have removed Me as their plumb line for Truth and barely recognize what sin is. They think anything goes. But whether they recognize their sin or not, My Truth has not changed with the times and it is still sin. And, whether they think it or do it makes no difference in My sight.

However, forgiveness is the key. As I forgive you, you in turn must learn to forgive others as well as yourself. When you love as I love, you can only forgive because it is My Nature not to condemn. Yes, you will sin, but through My Love for you, I freely give you forgiveness. My Blood covers all. And, as you strive to be more like Me as I become more a part of you, this same forgiveness must be extended from you to others. You see, My true Love will not allow you to do otherwise.

November 17

Wonder of wonders I AM. As we share more together, you will begin to see My Hand in everything. You will see what you thought a coincidence before was merely another part of My perfect plan. And, even though you know on some level that I am your all, you will still be amazed at My attention to detail, My perfection. Look for Me more and more as I take charge of all, and rejoice in the wonder of our relationship.

Most are unaware of My ability and My desire to handle *all* sweetly. So many think I could care less about what goes on in their lives, if they even acknowledge My Existence at all. Help them to see My kindness and compassion toward them by opening their eyes to what they have called "coincidence", so they understand that I am their *coincidence*. Their God I AM.

November 18

The Mercy Seat does not close for certain sins and stay open for other sins which the world views as lesser. A sin is a sin is a sin. Whether in thought or in deed, it remains a sin. Many of My children believe it is not bad if they think it but do not do it. Of course, once you act out your sinful thought, you may have to suffer the consequences of those actions. But, in My Eyes, one sin is as another. There are not categories of sins as some people would have you believe. If I told you it was a sin, then it is a sin without qualification.

But, the important thing is... *I forgive all.* If you throw yourself before the Mercy Seat, I forgive all. First, realize you have sinned, which many now do not because they have classified sins into better or worse or dismissed them totally. Then, ask for My forgiveness and you will have it. Do not deceive yourself. You are not perfect and will sin, but I have accounted for that and *will always* forgive you, *have always* forgiven you.

November 19

Listen for My Voice... be obedient... spread the Good News... and I will handle all. So many in loving Me and desiring to tell others of Me, forget or are unaware that they should move under My direction. Without it, they often do more harm than good. Yes, you must spread My Word. But, first learn to listen to Me so you know what to say, how to say it and when to say it. Remember when I said to have no concern for what you will say, for the words will be there? Well, that is an example of how I expect My Gospel to be spread. I will give you the message/the words, and they will always be perfect.

Listen for Me first for all direction, then be obedient. The rest will come as you and I journey together.

November 20

> **When I was a child, I spoke as a child, I understood as a child, I thought as a child; but when I became a man, I put away childish things (1 Corinthians 13:11 – NKJV).**

Many of My children are unwilling to put away those childish things and that is why they are unable to mature/grow in Me. I need My children to be mature, to know My Word, to speak it and do it. We have no time for childish games. Time is short and people must be saved. Read My Word... listen to Me... then act. You have nothing to fear. Take My Word and run with it like the Olympic runner with the torch!

I am no respecter of persons. I will use and teach whoever desires it. Your will, your removal of self and the depth of your love will determine the intensity of that use – not necessarily to be seen by the outside world in large groups, but seen in how I use you daily to minister to others. Be mindful of this. The large crowds and public recognition received without Me in the midst, do not please Me as much as when you are moving in My perfect will in whatever the size of the group.

November 21

I *do* take care of all your needs. Never ever doubt that because it is your doubt that interferes with My miracle-working power. Stand on My Word and walk in faith. Even those who do not know I am in charge are being cared for. Praise Me!

Never feel/believe that something is too great for Me to handle. For in thus thinking, you limit Me and My ability to work My greatest miracles. I am not such that I run rough-shod over you or force you to do things that are distasteful to you. No, you make the choice always. Even when I change your heart so your attitude is different, it is always after/only after you have made a choice to serve Me in some way. Your choices release Me or bind Me. Make the choice to let My Love and power flow freely as we travel this life together. Make the choice to know I can *indeed* do all things.

November 22

And though I bestow all my goods to feed the poor, and though I give my body to be burned, and have not love, it profits me nothing (1 Corinthians 13:3 – NKJV).

Love is My Message to the universe, for without love, My kind of love, you have nothing. All of your works and activities are nothing if they are not based in the fullness of love. Each day dwell on the thought of how you can do each thing/everything in love. Practice it until it becomes such a part of you that you make no conscious effort to do it. Then, only then, will you have tasted My Love, My real Love – My purity. Above all, love Me... and all other things will come into place. It is the order of My Kingdom – love for Me first. Open yourself to experience My Love more fully and you will see what it means to be Mine.

November 23

I have given you the key to My Heart. Unlock the door to My Love by immersing yourself in My Word and yielding to Me. I will provide all of your needs – the smallest to the absolute largest. The more you love and praise Me, the better it gets. And, because praise pleases Me so much, it greases the lock. It is so simple, so simple.

Many will fail in their search for happiness as they will not recognize the importance of Me for true happiness. It is such a simple formula. As you yield and love Me, I love, guide and protect you. I am not here to make life hard for you, for what would be the purpose of creating you? I am love. I am light. I am truth. Therefore, I am unable to do the evil of which I am so often accused. No father would do the evil things attributed to Me unless he was sick/Satan. I am perfection. Therefore, it would be impossible for Me to inflict such evil. Tell them. Many will not believe, but many will. Tell them.

November 24

My Word and My Body are to be one – never separated, always true, making all things possible as one. It is time for it to be so, as planned since the beginning.

Sharing My Love as one, united before the world, is how it was planned for you to be. There have been too many parts of the Body functioning on their own with individual interpretations of love. No! I make it clear what love is and how it should be demonstrated. Without My integral involvement, you shall have no positive influence on the world. But, with Me pulling each part together as one and guiding the total Body in love, we shall not only draw in those outside, but we shall rule in this world as was intended. Love, unite and yield yourself for the greater works of the Body.

November 25

> **I know thy works: behold, I have set before thee an open door, and no man can shut it:**

for thou hast a little strength, and hast kept my word, and hast not denied my name (Revelation 3:8 – KJV).

There is never any need to fear the unknown in your walk with Me, for when you know that I am in charge and handling all, you know the best is being worked out for you. You understand that through faith in Me, there is nothing unknown because I know all and am sharing with you as time goes on. Learn to walk in trust with Me, relying on My wisdom and knowledge. And, know there is no fear in Me.

Focus on Me. Focus on Me. Take not your eyes from Me and everything, everything will be in order. You never have to figure out what to do if you focus on Me for your answers. I want you to succeed, to do well, to do right, to walk as My child – so I have provided all you need to achieve these heights. My children must realize My purpose in creating them. Many are getting it now, though, and I am so glad!

Satan comes like a thief in the night. Watch for him.

November 26

"And where I go you know, and the way you know" (John 14:4 – NKJV).

Seldom shall people see Me face to face, but they will know Me by My Presence. Do not pray to see Me as one does in Heaven, but pray that you *know* Me. For if you truly know Me, you shall surely see Me. Although many are and will be saved, few will know Me truly... and know what they *really* have in and through Me.

I want My children to have it all, but many will never have it because they cannot translate it into their day-to-day lives. They *can* have the Kingdom on earth; but instead, they take just a small portion of it and think that is all they can have. I have it *all*... the entire thing... the whole ball of wax.

There is no reason for any of My children to be satisfied with a little. They are *My* children. My own Son died that they might have it all, so why would I not give them the Kingdom on earth – *My* Kingdom on earth? What do I mean by My Kingdom? First, it encompasses My Love, protection and guidance... then eternal life, abundance, joy, health, healing and wholeness. You are to have all that I have and through our relationship, you will dwell with Me forever.

November 27

Watching and waiting.

Watch Me work. Watch Me move as you never thought possible once you have left all to Me. Most know how to watch, but few know how to wait. This is an ingredient which you must have deeply ingrained within you to move as you need to move in My fullness. Wait and know I will move you at the absolute perfect time in a most perfect way. Watch and wait.

Cherish the thought of My Love for you. When all else fails and you are filled with doubt and fear, think of My precious

Love for you. Think about the intensity of My Love for you and know it would be impossible not to take care of you when filled with such love. The purity of My Love forces Me to do all you have the faith to believe I can do. Therein you find peace, in knowing My Love for you causes Me to work all together for your good, independent of your slips and falls. Dwell on this and rest in Me.

November 28

> **[1] Praise the Lord. Praise God in his sanctuary; praise him in his mighty heavens. [6] Let everything that has breath praise the Lord. Praise the Lord (Psalm 150:1, 6 – NIV).**

I have ordained that you should praise Me continually. When you praise, all of Heaven sings and rejoices with you. When you praise Me, it spills over onto others without their awareness. When you praise Me, you are not only declaring your love and adoration for Me, you are declaring war in the heavenlies with a war cry that causes the angels to stand ready to defeat the evil plans of My enemy. Paul and Silas understood this as they praised Me in their dungeon cell and were instantly loosed from their bonds.

Never let anyone tell you that praise is not for today. Never let anyone tell you that it does not require your complete involvement. Never let anyone persuade you that praise is not what I cherish. Never let anyone convince you that I do not do great works in the midst of your sincere, heart-felt praise.

November 29

Beloved, I wish above all things that thou mayest prosper and be in health, even as thy soul prospereth (3 John 2 – KJV).

When you love Me and focus on Me, it does not mean you will not encounter difficulties, for you surely will with My adversary roaming to and fro. But, you can rest assured he is already a defeated foe. The battle has already been fought in Heaven (Oh, it is a beautiful place!) and won. Praise Me! Continue to center yourself on Me, and the miracles which will occur will be beyond your wildest dreams. Take heed of My wishes, for they are there for a purpose.

Immediate obedience is what I must have to do My work through you. It may not seem important to you at the time, but you cannot see the total picture. I demand immediate obedience, for how can I increase your responsibilities if I cannot count on immediate submission from you? I need you to decrease so that I may increase. Then, you will be increased beyond anything you could ever have on your own.

November 30

Open your eyes and see the miracles each day – large ones or small ones, but *indeed* miracles. I will give them to each and every one of you, if you but let Me. Then recognize them.

As you study My Word and grow more used to them, it will become easier for you to expect bigger and better miracles. It is called "faith building"... the faith that I can do *all* things from the smallest to the largest.

Can you believe it? Well, believe it! There will be many miracles and with each one, your faith will grow and grow until you have Me in every part of your being. That is as it should be. If you keep your eyes on Me, you can do *all* things through Me.

In your walk of faith with Me, you cannot know all because where would be your faith? No, I reveal parts of a plan to you so you know a direction, a goal. But, in the unknown with Me, your growth of faith comes. For you know I am handling everything to your good and you become stronger in Me with that trust. Therefore, do not fret when things are unknown. Only allow your faith in Me to flow, knowing you and your future are secure in Me.

DECEMBER

December 1

Take heed of My every Word/Promise and stand on them. They are yours. That is the key to remaining strong in Me.

We are going to have a lot to do in a relatively short period of time, so be ready. It will be clear exactly what I want you to do, how I want you to do it and when I want you to do it, so stay tuned-in to Me, particularly now. Of course, you should always be tuned-in, prepared to hear My Voice and expect your miracles/blessings... *always*.

Concern yourself with Me and My plan to take the Word to the world – unsaved and lukewarm. Lukewarm is almost as "bad" as being unsaved, for what purpose do they serve? They have eternal life, but neither help themselves nor anyone else to draw nigh to Me. They have confined Me for centuries by not believing My Promises. It is time to show them the Truth. Get ready! Do not be sidetracked or give up just before it happens. Wait on Me. Wait on Me.

December 2

Manifest My Word in your every action. Those around you must know that I am in you – directing you, loving you, teaching you. They must know that by coming to Me through faith and love, they can have the same. Your life will be a testimony of what I can do through anyone who is Mine. They must know that nothing, nothing is impossible through Christ Jesus for those who know and love Me.

As you grow in Me, even tithing will very shortly have little application for you because you will be giving Me your all – your time, your energy, your money. When I say *all*, I do not mean you will not have what you need and want for yourself, for I am committed to caring for you. I am speaking of you in your entirety, so that giving will be of an *all* nature and not concerned with percentages. Begin now to manifest My Word by giving Me your *all*.

December 3

Complete faith and yielding – that is My Theme. Without them, I cannot do My work through you.

Manage your affairs well and you will have others to handle. I will provide everything, everything you need. Do not let certain people get to you as they are only tools/puppets of Satan without even knowing it. Continue to focus on Me and realize there is nothing beyond My reach or capability. Believe in Me. Love Me. Heed My Word and pray for those who treat you unkindly.

Do not be *I* oriented. Ego and greed have deterred many of My children who gave Me honor and glory originally. Ego and greed are extremely sly and cancerous twins that cause nothing but deceit, division and destruction. But, I will expose them, so be alert to them. Focus. Listen.

December 4

My Love is boundless. The more you love Me, the more you are aware of the limitless nature of My Love and power. I can do *all* things. Do you truly realize what that means? *All!* That means everything you have ever thought, are thinking, will ever think... I know and can do it. Expand your thinking to include all things in My power and with it your faith. Believe Me for everything. From your waking up to your going to sleep, count on Me for all things. I am *it*. There is nothing/no one else – no Mother Nature, no other gods. I am it... the beginning, the end and all in between. Praise Me!

Do not fret or worry. Continue to focus on Me. You shall have what I have ordained for you at the appointed time. Leave it to Me. It will be done. Continue to walk in faith and believe.

December 5

Listen to Me always. You may not understand the importance immediately, but listen and be aware of My guidance because everything works together for good to those who love Me. Do not allow yourself to be discouraged about anything, for you shall want for naught. I am your provider. All things come through Me. Look not to yourself for understanding, but to Me. I am all-knowing… all-powerful… and all-loving. I will show you all you need to know. I will provide for you. And, I will love you through Eternity.

Eternity – being with Me through Eternity… ad infinitum… forever. It will be beautiful – loving, sharing, full of light. Tell the people of the beauty of My loving relationship. Miracles!

Do you really love Me as you say you do? Well, why do you not allow Me to care for you as lovers do? You tell Me you love Me and then you fret, if ever so slightly. Or something is moving too slowly and you get impatient, if just for a moment. If you love Me as you say you do, then turn yourself over to Me totally, without exception, and I will be your champion in every cause.

December 6

Day to day your spirit and Mine are as one and you will know whether to do or not to do. As long as you seek Me, the peace that is needed to act will be an essential factor before you are able to act. I will always be there for counsel. Do not go ahead of Me and it will be clear what should and should not be done. Seek Me moment by moment.

We are in the days when My people are to unite in My Name and go forth carrying My power, My wisdom, My Love. There are too many lost and it is because the Church has not reached out to them. I care not for these buildings in which much time, energy and money are invested. I care about My lost… those who need to be drawn into the flock. Church is and should be where people are gathered together in My Name/where I am. It could be in a field, a forest or even a barn.

Being concerned about and prideful of buildings and the size of the congregation is not what I intended. The size of the congregation is only important if it increases the number of people who are reaching out to the lost. It has nothing to do with being comfortable inside their beautiful buildings, behind their seen and unseen walls saying, "Praise the Lord!" I can barely hear them compared to someone serving Me – at home, at work, in the community, overseas or wherever they may be.

December 7

> **...that I may know Him and the power of His resurrection, and the fellowship of His sufferings, being conformed to His death (Philippians 3:10 – NKJV).**

I care not as much for the final outcomes as I do with where your heart is, the state of your heart. Yes, you will do things wrong – often without realizing it and sometimes realizing it – because you are not perfect. But, because of My Love for you, I forgive and *forget*. The souls that you bring to Me will show Me where your heart really is.

My Love is not a condemning, judgmental love, but rather a love that will teach and guide while not nearly as concerned with your stumbles as with your large strides. Often with each slip, you get stronger knowing how to fight particular temptations. It is not an easy, no-challenges road. But, since I have already fought the battles, it is a road on which you are victorious. And, all along the way, you will find Me. Praise Me! Praise Me!

Love, health and joy are what I want for you. I never meant for you to be without love, sick or sad. I never meant for it to be that way.

December 8

> **After that, He poured water into a basin and began to wash the disciples' feet, and to wipe *them* with the towel with which He was girded (John 13:5 – NKJV).**

Service.

Service is so important for My children. To really see the beauty of My Kingdom, you must first serve. You serve in order to be served. Did I not wash the feet of My disciples and now sit in the Throne Room? Well, you can do no less. You are called to become less before you become more.

Pride and ego have no place in My Kingdom. You must decrease so that I may increase, then you will be exalted. I need your service with a humble heart because I cannot work when there is pride – a prideful spirit – even when it is related to My Kingdom work. There is no way for Me to be in control if you are patting yourself on the back about how well you are doing or what you know. Always ask how can you serve Me. I know there is pleasure in growth, but growth is not to boast. Growth has been the downfall of many because their focus changed. Watch carefully and never exalt yourself.

Some of My children are willing to grow and others are not. Do not agonize over it, but be ready to intercede and provide support for them. As you continue to grow, there will be union with many, but separation from even more.

December 9

Knowing Jesus.

It is so important for you to *know* Me and not just know of Me. I am not able to provide you with My Promises when you think of Me as some distant force handling all the big problems of the world. I am with you and meant to be *in* you. I want you to have everything I have promised. But, until you stretch your understanding of Me, I am limited in what I can accomplish. I am love, peace and all things true. Come to know Me.

Too often men profess to know Me, but have no idea of what I am about other than the basics that have been taught over the years – forgiveness of sins, salvation. My children perish for lack of knowledge. Let nothing interfere with your mission to take My Word to the flock – discouragement or criticism or lack of support should not deter you. This mission is bigger than anyone's feelings, so do not lose sight of My plan. My Word must be available for all – rich or poor, black, white or beige, inner city or suburbs, denominational or non-denominational.

Time is growing short and My adversary has pulled out all of the stops. So, beware at all times by resting/trusting in Me and walking in faith. Separation is not what I am about, unless it has to do with the adversary.

December 10

In old Jerusalem, the people were "good" people – misguided, but good. They had their chores to do, lived pretty much according to traditions set forth by their forefathers and had what others would consider a good life. Often people today are "good" people, but they have so missed My Calling, they are dead without knowing it. Many of them are even better acting than My so-called flock – the heathen act better than the Christians. This must change! Christians must show their love in everyday ways, or what will draw the unsaved to Me?

You are to go forth *boldly* doing good in My Name – boldly as Jesus would, filled with love and fearful for naught. *Go forth boldly with love!*

December 11

I wish that all might be lovers of Me, themselves and others. Love is the key to the Kingdom – love, faith, quick obedience and removal of self.

I would have you do My work without worry or strife. I would have you carry My Love to all. I would have you cherish the love that I have for you. I would have you do My work at all times. A sweet smile, a tender word can be all that is required at any given time. I would have My Love flow through your humble spirit to touch all around you.

This is manifestation of My ministry. What happens beyond that is the icing on the cake. Understand that the ministry which I have placed in your hand is only part of My work for you. I want you to *live* Me. I have so many who are tarnished in My Family and do not know the solution for cleaning them is Me… quickly, as cleaning tarnished silver vessels. Show them what it means to live Me – holy and untarnished.

December 12

> **And we know that in all things God works for the good of those who love him, who have been called according to his purpose (Romans 8:28 – NIV).**

Never test Me, but in seeking Me, it is correct to ask for clarity as to what I would have you do. There is a difference between saying, "If You make this clear, I will know to do this," and saying, "I am going to do thus and such, and You show me that it is You."

Believe that I am in all situations. If you make a wrong judgment while you are yet seeking Me, it will be taken care of. Did I not tell you all things work together for good to those who love Christ Jesus? Well then, continue to seek Me for your answers and in so doing you will become more proficient in the interpretation of My direction. Focus... Focus... Focus.

I love you, each and every one, so much! Things of Satan can always be changed/revised when I am involved, really involved. Praise Me! Praise Me!

December 13

Shall we meet on High?

My children shall be caught up in the air to dwell with Me in Paradise! Satan is getting very anxious because he knows his time is drawing nigh. That is why he is more visible than ever, and My Word is as well. But, many are still unaware of what is happening. Therefore, work unceasingly to inform them of My Love and everything I have for them, as well as what can await them on the other side – the eternal damnation of Hell. It is time for them to realize that this is the most serious decision they will ever have to make. It is for Eternity.

Do not be concerned about how it has been missed over the years, only concern yourself with bringing the lost to Me. Continue on. Never get stuck on the things you have missed and think yourself foolish, stupid or even bad.

Your finances are an obvious target for Satan as he tries to steal your joy and cause confusion. Jobs, bills... the world is so based on the money system, he knows it is an excellent place to attack. Do not worry or take your focus from Me. He is the loser. You are the winner and I have already decreed it! The power you have in Me will blow your mind as you continue to exercise it!

December 14

Blessed are those who walk down My path. Blessed are those who seek My Face. Blessed are those who love their brothers and sisters as they love themselves. Blessing upon blessing have I for you if you but believe My Promises and walk in love.

You would think people would want to be surrounded by love and light, but My adversary has so blinded them, they do not even know they are not in the light. They do not even know what the God kind of Love is.

Remove the blinders from their hooded eyes and show them My message of love and light. Show them through sharing, teaching and example how they can share in My Kingdom/My Promises – how to walk in faith and believe My Word.

December 15

I would have you build My Kingdom here on earth so that all may dwell with Me forever. There is no reason for people to wait until they shed their physical bodies to dwell in My Kingdom. They are to dwell in it now. That was how I purposed it, so they could dwell with Me spiritually while in this life. The power, love and peace available to them is all but missed by most. Spread My Word and tell them of My Glory here on earth.

There are many things you will not get right along the way. But, as you continue to stay in Me and read My Word/the Truth, those things will become fewer and fewer. Praise Me!

Many will come and many will go, but My Word stands forever. So, continue to stand on it. Discouragement, frustration, confusion… they are just ways to separate you from Me. Do not fall for the tricks of the enemy. Recognize them and return your focus to Me because everything is according to plan. Tunnel vision is what I want from you. A single mind is what I must have – humility without ego. Take it from there and hold tight. You will see many miracles, so be ready!

December 16

> **O taste and see that the Lord is good: blessed is the man that trusteth in him (Psalm 34:8 – KJV).**

I will build a people who know their *true* power in Me, who will take My Word to the world. You are to be in that group, fully exercising your authority in Me. I have so much to offer My children yet so little has been taken. It is like a delicious cherry pie in which only the crust around the edge of the pan has been eaten, leaving all of the delicious fruit on the inside untouched. That is how My children have been. They have left all of the wonderful cherry filling (the power of the Holy Spirit) virtually untouched.

My entire plan is based on your taking what is rightfully yours as a gift from Me. So, cut that pie and savor the wonderful filling until you are full. Then, come back for more once it is digested. I have more than enough to satisfy your hunger. There will always be more to learn, more ways to grow, more power. More... more... more. Taste and see just how good I am! You will not be greedier than I permit because I want you to have it all.

Trust Me for *all* your needs – money, love, direction, growth. *All.* Therein lies the power, My power.

December 17

I would build a people who are not afraid to take My Word boldly to the masses. Time is growing short and there is no time for hesitancy, lack of commitment or confusion. I am here to make everything clear to you for action. Those people who say that speaking in tongues is the ultimate for salvation or doing My work are mistaken, and you must boldly tell them. I even work through sinners in order to bring them to Me. How could I do that if it were not for My Holy Spirit being able to influence them, if only briefly?

And what of all My workers who have never spoken in tongues but truly love Me and believe. Of course My Spirit is in them, but not manifested in tongues. I did not say that everyone would speak in tongues or everyone who spoke in tongues was saved and truly filled. They must stop this nonsense about tongues. Yes, it has a place, a great place that brings understanding, strength and intimacy. But, it is not the end all. It is barely the beginning. Do they have love and compassion one for another? Do they have peace? Do they have joy? Do they walk in holiness and wisdom?

They must stop getting stuck on this issue and unite themselves with other Christians, instead of believing their way/their understanding is the *only* way. Stand firm. My Spirit is in each of you. But, until you exercise Him and grow in My gifts and My power, He seems not to be present. He *is*, however.

December 18

Take My Hand and walk with Me. Through Me you can enter all doors because there is nothing closed to you. From miracles to entering the Court of My Father, nothing is closed to you.

People must stop bickering and instead, be concerned about maturing as Christians. Most get saved and think that is it. But, they need to know there is so much more. Only a mature Christian can reap My fullest rewards. Continue to confess My Word and the manifestations will surprise even you. There is so much to do and so little time to do it.

We sing here not only when a soul is saved, but when we see that baby Christian taking steps forward in My Word. The smallest or the largest step forward is reason to rejoice. Continue to go forward, for through Me you can do all things and nothing, nothing is impossible to you.

December 19

Go forth in My Name and speak My Word boldly providing interpretation. You will dream dreams with their interpretations and see visions with the same. Share them with others. Always be aware of Satan's interference with the delivery of the Message, but do not fear because you have My protection and power to erase him. The revelations in your spirit will continue to grow, so do not be frightened as to hamper, but let them flow. In doing so, others will expand their expectations as to what they can do through Me.

Do not consider Me some plaything to do your bidding. I am King of kings and Lord of lords, ready to provide you with My Promises as you come boldly to My Father's Throne, but not without reverence and respect for our relationship.

Then shall the eyes of the blind be opened, and the ears of the deaf unstopped. You are to serve this purpose – to bring light to the eyes of those who are in darkness that they may see, and help others to hear My Voice and know My joy. As you grow, you will touch more and more people. More than you will ever know. I will bless you as you move in My Name. I will bless you and bless you. That is My Promise to you.

December 20

> **The Lord is my shepherd; I shall not want (Psalm 23:1 – KJV).**

I will strike you with the power of the Holy Spirit to be an inspiration to all around you. Yes, it places more pressure on you, but the pressure can be as smooth as glass if you depend on Me. Remember, I am in control. People need to see the example of a Christian dealing with the day-to-day challenges of the world, but handling them in a totally different way – by turning them over to Me. You will reach that goal.

Time is so important to you in your daily life, but it really means so little in the scheme of things. Were you to see the total picture, you would understand. They pierced Me thinking it would put an end to Me. Little did they know it contributed to My Father's total plan of victory. I died for you – your burdens, your anxieties, your pain, your sickness, your salvation. I died for it all. So, turn it all over to Me, for there is no reason for you to experience it again. It is already done!

December 21

Joy to the world!

My birth signaled a new beginning for mankind. That I was made flesh and walked among man was the beginning, but that I died and sit at the Right Hand of My Father, is the culmination of that birth. So many people place more emphasis on My birth than on the importance of My death. That I had to die to sit in petition for you with My Father, is where your eyes should hold their focus. Your new birth, which only comes through My Resurrection, is the Foundation upon which the Church should be based.

I your God, am the Beginning and the End and all that occurs in between. I do take care of all things. Do you realize the magnitude of that? I take care of *all* things; from the operation of the universe to each hair on your head, from worldwide concerns to whether you catch a taxi or not. Receive My gift to handle it all – health, money, happiness, work, ministry.

December 22

> **Be it known unto you all, and to all the people of Israel, that by the name of Jesus Christ of Nazareth, whom ye crucified, whom God raised from the dead, even by him doth this man stand here before you whole (Acts 4:10 – KJV).**

They must know of My power. I can heal all situations. I can heal the physically impaired, the emotionally ill and the mentally diseased. I can repair finances, any weakness or infirmity. This is My power. My Son died so that all men can be made whole. Exercise this same power with others so they may go forth. I have given you this charge.

I am the Alpha and the Omega. I have no limits except through you. Tell them to release all their cares to Me and receive My miracle-working power to My Glory. Seeing you walk in faith while exercising My Love and power, is the best example possible. Then, when you get their attention, you give them the big whammy – *My Word*. We must get their attention and then move in. If this sounds like warfare, it is. But, we have already fought the battle and won!

All you have to do is receive what has been given to you. You shall not fear. You shall walk in faith. *All* of the battles have been fought and won. Remember that. The Sword of the Spirit/ My Word and your Shield of Faith shall comfort and protect you. *Glory to God!*

December 23

I will impart My wisdom and knowledge to any who desire it. But, in doing so, you are then placed under greater responsibility to use them in Jesus' Name to reach others. You cannot/ may not receive the mysteries of My wisdom and knowledge without acting upon them, only to tell others you have them. I wish that each one of you would receive My gifts so we can slay Satan now, once and for all. However, it is not so at this time.

Then shall the eyes of the blind be opened and ears of the deaf unstopped. We are in a time when the eyes of many will be unveiled and they will be able to see Me for the first time, hear Me speak to them with recognition for the first time. You must help them to do this. Show them by example and through the Word how I can cause them to see and hear as they never have before.

December 24

My way should be your way. There should be no other way. Continue to teach others about Me by showing the importance of having Me in *each* part of their lives. There can be no segmentation, if you are to truly walk in the Spirit. Do not be concerned about looking fanatical just because you are around different people. Continue to speak My Word, as the angels sing! Continue to be bold – not pushy, not over-talkative – but bold in the things you say.

Peace I bring to you now, not later when I come again, but now. "Peace on earth" means partaking of the peace I have for you in every situation. You can choose to worry, but why, when I am the peace that flows through all things. Think of what "peace on earth" means. It is not just a world without war and fighting. It is your peace within which flows to the outside. Without the peace of your spirit first, there can be no external manifestation. Peace begins with Me and flows through you for your use and then distribution to others for their use.

December 25

> **For unto you is born this day in the city of David a Saviour, which is Christ the Lord (Luke 2:11 – KJV).**

Yes, My Day… a day when much of the world worships Me, although in a somewhat backhanded way. Nonetheless, it does put many in remembrance of Me, if only briefly. Remember the Babe in the manger who grew up without sin to fulfill His Destiny – death – so that you might live… to carry the sins of the world on His Shoulders… to see His Father's Back so you might be cleansed… then, to sit at the Right Hand of His Father so you might live eternally… and finally, to dwell in you so you might live with Him in power. Glory! Glory!

It has been a year of tremendous growth, but it is only the beginning. Touch each and every one with My Story, never condemning yourself when someone does not receive it. You cannot make anyone receive. You can only provide the means. My Story, the only Story, the greatest Story for mankind… and most do not know it, truly know it.

December 26

You will walk as I walk… do as I do. When it is time to move, you will move, as I am in you and you will know. If it is unclear, do not move. I am not unclear.

You cannot go by what other people say. Go by what I say and believe that I will guide you. Did I not guide My people out of Egypt? And, if they had kept their focus on Me, I would have done it quickly. However, they did not trust Me and it took forty years to take a trip which should have taken a few days. Keep your focus on Me so that our trip can be accomplished in a timely fashion. I know how to lead you. Do not try to figure it out. Just be submissive and follow Me.

You need not be concerned about agreement with others on the small points, but there must be no compromise on Me, My Love and My direction. On certain things, there can be no compromise, for would I compromise with Satan? No! Salvation, your walk, My power, My Love – on these issues there can be no compromise – but, the works/traditions must be overlooked at times for the greater purpose. When they are not to be, you will know. I am not unclear. Only the limits of your mind make things unclear.

December 27

...and, lo, I am with you always, even unto the end of the world (Matthew 28:20 – KJV).

Seek My Face always as I am with you always, even until the end of the earth. I will never leave you nor forsake you. Realize I am with you, in you and through you. So, you need never feel alone or lost, because I am with you always and do not plan to lose one of you, no not one. When you think I am gone, it is simply that you have lost the assurance of My Presence or are not seeking Me, but I am there. I am and will always be there.

The enemy will attempt to distract you and try to make you think I have deserted you, but do not succumb to him. Be forewarned as you must do your part. There is always a part that you must play in moving My plan through to its perfect completion.

December 28

So much is lost to you for lack of faith. If you cannot believe, how can you expect to receive the miracles that are released through your belief? Of course, I can do all things.

But, My choice is to do them based on your faith for your growth to the Glory of the Father. I will always bless you, but often throughout your growth, you do not recognize them as gifts from Heaven. As you mature, I desire the recognition to increase what I do for you. Realize you are not a robot waiting to be acted upon. Know you have an integral role and I have awaited your actions since before time began.

I would have you go forth in My Word, looking neither to the right nor the left as I and My Holy Spirit guide you. Walk forward in My Name, know My Voice, stand on My Word. Above all, recognize Me in even the smallest things, for how else can I guide you? And, how do you recognize Me? By seeking Me through My Word and the Holy Spirit.

You have the power to reach all heights through Me. Expand… expand. Recognize Me for who I *am* and the adversary for who he is *not*. All things will come to you if you but wait on Me. Wait on Me. Teach My people that they can do all things through Me as I manifest Myself.

December 29

Do you think I forget you just because you err? You are My child. Does a loving earthly parent turn his back on his child when he/she falters or makes a mistake? Of course not. Then why, as the Father of everlasting love, do you not expect at least the same from Me? Yes, I expect each of you to walk in the Spirit, but I know also that you are imprisoned in flesh. Therefore, I also know even with My Holy Spirit indwelling you, there are constant battles. Be victorious in My Spirit and as you grow faithfully, so will your victories. I am your *God of love*... I know your heart. Do not ever expect less of Me than a natural parent, for I am so much more. What you have seen is a glimpse of what I have in store for all of My children, just a glimpse. There is so much more.

Come grow with Me and learn more of Me, My Love and My power. I came not to condemn those who love Me, but to raise them to the heights of My Kingdom here on earth and forevermore. Do not give up on yourself when you fall short of Me. It will always be until you are with Me in Paradise. I have not chosen you for your works. Remember that. I have chosen you because I *love* you. Be strong and bold in My Son's Name – not strong willed – and all shall come to sing My praises. Shout and sing with joy – claims of Truth for the world to see!

December 30

My Body is meant to be married to one another... moving as one... married to Me with no separation. Open your eyes to this kind of marriage. Marriage is the ultimate union exemplified first by you/My Bride and Me, then by a husband and wife. But it does not stop there. My Body must be married in the true sense of the word, walking as one, joined spirit to spirit. In these latter days, it must be so.

I will not and cannot tolerate separation among My Body. Those who would ignore the teaching given through My Word and My Spirit will have to pay the consequences. When I return, I cannot have people who would cause division in My Kingdom. They will have to yield to My leading or be left outside of My Court.

December 31

My Life and your life are one. The pain you feel is magnified in Me an hundredfold as is your sorrow and disappointment. The same is true of your joy and happiness, with the difference being all of Heaven sings with you then. Seeing My children full of joy makes the sting of your sorrow and pain at other times, much easier to bear. Strive for more joy, which will bless you as you bless Me.

I am the Lord your God. I know and see all things. I know what has happened, what will happen and what is happening now. Your time frames are not always received as they are given, but they will always be in perfect time. Do not worry or fret about any of it. What I have planned for you will reach fruition shortly. Everything is as it should be – do not concern yourself. Only continue to listen to Me and seek My Face as you move in love, My Love.

Let no one come to Me except through My Son, Jesus. Be ready. Walk as I walk and love as I love. I am filling you with My Love to the point of almost bursting, so your love will overflow to others who have never known My Love. *Go forth… go forth, My child!*

Look For

Listen, My Child

Ears to Hear Series Book 2

Coming Soon!

CPSIA information can be obtained
at www.ICGtesting.com
Printed in the USA
LVOW12s0512140317
527019LV00001B/1/P